"*Marvelous* is an inspiring collection of true stories that will touch your heart and deepen your faith. Every page is a powerful reminder that we are surrounded by the miracles of answered prayer."

—Alice Gray, Speaker/Author. Creator and compiler of the award winning book series *Stories for the Heart*

"In a culture filled with skepticism and surplus, *Marvelous* is a poignant reminder that the Lord is still working in miraculous ways to bring healing and redemption. I can't wait to share these stories with my children, so they can see the mighty power of prayer!"

—JJ Heller, Singer/Songwriter

"Prayer is amazing! Yet we so easily forget its power and influence. *Marvelous* reminds us of God's miraculous interventions in our everyday life. It also challenges us to go to Him more often. These stories will change your life. You will find yourself reflecting on them and sharing them with others long after you've put the book down. I can't wait to read the sequel."

—Dr. Steve Stephens, Author/Professor/Psychologist, with more than 28 books in print

"For a healthy dose of faith, inspiration, and a renewed yearning to pray more...read this book!"

—Doug Batchelor, President/Speaker, Amazing Facts

"These honest, real life stories of God's love and power intersecting lives, enlarged my faith and inspired me to believe God for more. *Marvelous* is marvelous!"

—John C. Ogle, Vice President of Development, Luis Palau Association

"Compelling, believable, refreshing! Along with the thrill of each slice of time when God intervened, the sheer literary finesse of the compiler was most refreshing!"

—Herbert Edgar Douglass, Th.D.

"Reading these amazing stories is like drinking a tall cool glass of hope. Each story increased my level of faith into believing that more of the impossible and miraculous will happen. The joy-filled endings pointed me to a loving Father and a Savior whose resurrected power still operates today."

—Dee Howell, Intercessor/Author, Adivineexchange.org

"There is nothing more powerful than prayer and *Marvelous—Amazing Stories of Answered Prayer* has dozens of personal, life-changing examples confirming this truth. I plan to give a copy of it to all of our prayer leaders at The Hollywood Prayer Network. The more we hear about others' answered prayers, the more our faith will grow!"

—Karen Covell, Producer/Founding Director, The Hollywood Prayer Network, www.hollywoodprayernetwork.org

"This book will encourage and inspire you to persevere in prayer, as story after story gives testimony of God's mighty hand in the lives of those who call on His name."

—Mary-Alice DeBoer, Director of Women's Ministries, Hinson Church

"This book vividly reminded me that throughout my everyday life, I am bathed in the miraculous presence of God Almighty. By reading (and re-reading again) these stories, I am joyously drawn into the light of God and His undergirding support. Everyone who reads this collection will celebrate God's wonder and loving care."

—Deborah A. Peterson, M.S., Grant Writing Consultant

"Wow! Christ followers know He answers prayer, but to relive so many examples stirs it out of the head into the heart. After each story I wanted to shout, "It's true! It's true!" May reading these 'answered prayers' encourage you to take a step of faith and let Him answer yours."

—Ted Noble, Retired President, Greater Europe Mission, U.S. Chair, Africa Inland Mission

"Story after story this book sent chills down my spine and gave me a sense of urgency to get down on my knees and pray. You will feel inspired and will not want to put this book down."
—Wendy Carter, National Account Executive

"From a child praying for a horse to a man helping a child with hypothermia to a woman bringing split pea soup to a neighbor with cancer, these real-life stories draw you in and make you smile. Every heart-grabbing narrative reminds you that God is the center and peace of our everyday world, if we'd only let Him be."
—Cornelia Becker Seigneur, Author of *Writer Mom Tales* and *Images of America: West Linn*, and Founder of the Faith and Culture Writers' Conference

"*Marvelous* is more than 'marvelous'...it's a tremendous blessing of a book. The compilation of short stories are powerful testimonials, and God stirred my heart with inspiration as I read them—of how He works through each of us."
—Sandy Liarokos, Cancer Center Fundraising Executive

"*Marvelous* is a collection of personal essays on answered prayer that cannot help but encourage readers. The contributors have experienced God at work in situations ranging from life-and-death experiences, to the ordinary occurrence of finding pennies on the ground. Yet these stories invariably attest to the reality that God is, He is personal and loving, and He cares for all His children."
—Alan and Pauly Heller, Co-founders, Walk and Talk Ministries

"This is a powerful book of testimonies. I was inspired by the persistence and growing faith of those who prayed for years before seeing answers. You will find yourself pondering and remembering the stories of how God answered those who prayed, and even how He pursued those who did not."
—Ann Tsen, M.D., Physician/Professional Coach

MARVELOUS - Amazing Stories of Answered Prayer
Compiled by: Suzanne Frey

Publisher: Frey Resource Group, LLC

Executive Editor: Suzanne Frey

Managing Editor: Lauren Frey

Editorial Assistance: Carey Chmarny, Ron Frey, David Sanford

Cover Design: Anneli Anderson, www.DesignAnneli.com

www.AmazingAnsweredPrayers.com

ISBN: 0692303421
ISBN 13: 9780692303429
Library of Congress Control Number: 2014917770
Marvelous, Happy Valley, OR

MARVELOUS

—

Amazing Stories of Answered Prayer

Suzanne Frey
Compiler and Executive Editor

My deepest gratitude to...

My family—Ron, Stephen, Lauren, and Katie—for believing in me and in this project. Your ideas and encouragement, as well as the countless hours of editing and assistance, have been invaluable.

My Mom's In Prayer friends, whom I've had the privilege of praying with for the past several years. Together, we've experienced the joy of pouring our hearts out to God, and have seen Him, in incredible and unforgettable ways, answer our prayers.

My Toastmasters friends in Noon Talkers and Abundant Talkers clubs. You have taught me the power of telling a story well, and helped me learn how to tell mine with skill and confidence.

My extended family and friends—thank you for your ongoing love, support, and prayers. I am so very blessed.

Each of the contributors who have shared your stories with courage, transparency, and integrity—this book could not have happened without you and your faith.

Jesus, knowing You and experiencing Your love, is the greatest joy in my life.

Contents

Introduction

When my three children were very young, our family traveled to Washington D.C. to visit its famous monuments and memorials. In preparation for our trip, we checked out books from the library—picture and historical fact books—and immersed ourselves in the history of each memorial and its significance to our nation. We felt this was one way we could truly appreciate what our eyes would be beholding.

We recognized that these monuments tell stories—important stories.

But the idea of building monuments to remember past events is nothing new.

In the Old Testament, God told His people to build memorials around significant events or miraculous signs of deliverance He performed for them. These establishments were not only serving as significant reminders to the nation of Israel, but were also meant to hold meaning to the surrounding tribes and countries, stating "This is who our God is" for future generations. Throughout the Old Testament, authors would note "And that stone is still there today."

Psalm 145:4-6 (MSG) says:

Generation after generation stands in awe of Your work;
Each one tells stories of Your mighty acts.
Your beauty and splendor have everyone talking...

*Your **marvelous** doings are headline news;*
I could write a book full of the details of your greatness.

And so the title of this book, *Marvelous*, was born out of this verse.

It is my hope that as you read these stories, you will walk with the contributors through the unique, challenging, and sometimes heart-wrenching circumstances, as they talked with God and trusted Him for the outcome.

My heart for this book is that it would share that same purpose of placing value on the testimonies of God, so much so, that we write them down, we build a memorial, we stop to pause and reflect and remember Who it is that loves us, and in what *marvelous* ways He does.

May God bless you in your journey.

Suzanne Frey

Editor's Note

Dear Reader,

The goal of this book is to tell accurate, interesting, and God-honoring stories of divine answers to human prayer. Due to the personal detail involved in some of these stories, names may have been replaced with pseudonyms or with their initials, where the contributors and I felt anonymity was essential.

We hope you will be encouraged by the words of each of these contributors; may their journeys lead you to better know and love the most important Character in their stories.

1

The Jungle Horse
Jerry Long

One day, my 10-year-old daughter Lori came to me and said: "Daddy, when I grow up, I want to raise horses. Can I have a horse?" At the time, my family and I were living in Limoncocha, the jungle center of operations for the Wycliffe Bible Translators in Ecuador.

"A horse?!" I thought. Living in the Amazon, she already had every animal imaginable. One day I counted 17 critters in, around, under and swinging from the rafters of our house. A calf from the local farm project was staked out in our backyard and there was an alligator in my shower stall.

"Honey," I said, "first of all, we can't afford a horse. Even if we could, the only way into our community is by boat or airplane. So the only way a horse could get here is either by flying or swimming. Besides, I don't know if horses can adapt to the jungle. They don't strike me as jungle animals."

Lori cried. She *really* wanted a horse.

So I said: "Honey, if you want a horse that bad, you need to talk to God about it. He's the only one I know who can arrange it."

So Lori took my advice and talked to God.

A few weeks later, I was handed a teletype message from Quito, the capital city of Ecuador, addressed to our neighbor, Otto Rodrigues, who had a hacienda—a large estate—about 30 miles upriver. The letter was from his attorney, telling him he needed to get into the city as soon as possible for some business transactions. It looked urgent enough that

I asked one of our pilots to fly me over to Otto's place so I could do a message drop.

As we flew over Otto's property, I noticed a horse grazing among his cattle. I thought: "How about that! There's a horse that survives in the jungle. I'll have to tell Lori."

About a week later, one of our Indian workers came to my door.

"Sr. Long," he said, "you won't believe what is coming down the river. There is a raft made of two dugout canoes with a platform on them—a platform with a *horse* tied on it."

A little later that day, a man came to my door leading the horse. He said: "Don Otto so appreciates his friends here at the mission that he sent this horse, thinking the kids would enjoy having him."

For the rest of our time at Limoncocha, Lori spent nearly all her days with that horse. This was God's gift to her. Today she boards, breeds and trains Arabian horses on her property in Oregon. But better yet, she still believes in prayer.

"Ask and it will be given to you; seek and you will find;
knock and the door will be opened to you."
Matthew 7:7

———

2

The Occult Store

As told to Priscilla Shirer

J aye Martin is a mother who lives in Houston, Texas. When I met her, I was captivated as she shared the story about a "store" that opened near her child's elementary school. The shop was known for selling merchandise connected to the occult. In addition to this, she and others in the community were fairly certain that illegal drugs were also being sold there.

At the time, Jaye was a part of a mom's prayer group that prayed for the protection of their children—children who spent much of their day close to that store. When they discovered that some of the children were wandering over there after school, and becoming interested in all of its wares, Jaye went to see the storeowner to express her concern.

The storeowner assured her there was no harm in what he was offering and otherwise ignored her. Despite her request that they find a location better suited to them and the community, they refused to leave.

Undeterred, she called the leasing agent and asked him to reconsider the lease because of the close proximity to the elementary school. He explained that he didn't see a reason not to allow them to rent space from him. Jaye, fed up with the obvious spiritual opposition, replied matter-of-factly: "Well then, we will just have to pray them out!"

At her next prayer meeting, she introduced the concept of not just praying for their children's safety, but praying the store out of the neighborhood. Honestly, the other mothers were stunned at this thought, as using prayer as a direction weapon was a new concept for many of them. But in faith, they prayed fervently that heaven would intervene on their behalf.

Two months later, the occultist store was gone.

"Truly I tell you that if two of you on earth agree about anything they ask for, it will be done for them by my Father in heaven."
Matthew 18:19

———

Used and edited with permission from Priscilla Shirer, *Anointed, Transformed and Redeemed*, LifeWay Publishers.

Priscilla Shirer is a speaker and author who has spent more than a decade addressing major corporations, organizations, and Christian audiences across the United States and around the world. Most recently Priscilla has focused on teaching the Bible to women through an expository teaching style. Her desire is to see women come to a full understanding of who they are in Christ by hearing the uncompromising truth of Scripture.

3

Powerless Statues
Guadalupe Gomez

The suffering began when I was 25 years old. The doctors told me the severe abdominal pain was gastritis, but as years dragged on, they found it was an ever-growing cyst in my bladder. The pain became so excruciating that for days, and sometimes weeks, I was completely unable to get out of bed. Doctors wanted to operate on me, to try and find all that was wrong with my body, but I was scared surgery would just make things worse. So I lived with the pain, extreme as it was. Many times it was so horrible I wanted to kill myself.

Now I have a total of seven children. All are grown, but two were born with intellectual disabilities and are unable to care for themselves. One night, after 20 years of pain, I was determined to take all of the pills I had. But once again, as every time before, I thought of these two children and decided to hold onto my life.

The next morning, a woman named Amanda came to my house. She was from Good Samaritan Ministries and had been hosting a Bible study every Wednesday morning for the women in my neighborhood, as well as counseling my daughter and me. She arrived early at my house and asked how I was doing. It was just the two of us, so I broke down crying and told her of my frustration with my pain.

"My never-ending pain is like living in hell," I said. "Because of the pain, I hate my life. And because of that, I've made mistakes that have hurt my family. And because of that, I feel unloved." I also told her of my hatred toward God and how I'd been rebelling against Him in sin.

Amanda prayed for me. She prayed for hope in my life. And as she did, the pain in my body began to leave! The next day, however, it started coming back.

Now I have many statues in my bedroom. A few nights later, I sat there in pain, considering again whether I should take my life. But instead, I decided to beg the statues of sacred saints to take away my physical agony. I prayed to the Virgin Guadalupe, to Saint Judas Todeo, and to the picture of the Lord of Mercy. I thought they represented God. But when they did nothing to alleviate the pain, I decided to stop praying to God and believing in Him altogether.

The next week, Amanda came again to my house for the Bible study and asked, "How are you, Guadalupe?"

"Not much better," I replied. "In fact, I've completely abandoned faith in God."

"Why?" she asked.

"I prayed to my statues to heal me. But they did not hear my prayers—God did not hear me."

"None of those are God," said Amanda. "You have to pray directly to God." Then Amanda showed me Deuteronomy 32:39 in the Bible, where it says that there is only one God and we are to pray to Him alone. And that He is not in a statue.

She had me place my hand over my stomach where it hurt, and she placed her hand on top of mine. Then she prayed to the One and Only True God, in the name of Jesus Christ, that He would heal my illness and take away the pain. In that moment, the pain started going away. I felt the power of God flow into me. I started feeling dizzy, and then I felt complete peace.

Not soon after, Amanda came to me and asked: "How are you doing, Guadalupe? How is the pain?" I gladly told her that the pain was completely gone, not only in that area, but throughout my whole body. I later went back to the doctor who had wanted to operate on me. He did an ultrasound and found that there wasn't a cyst in my bladder anymore.

After this healing, I now know the One True God, and I know that there is no other. I began telling people that there really is only One True God and to pray to Him alone.

Meanwhile, I have made many life-changing decisions in order to come closer to Christ. God has given me more patience with my children. I have stopped being rude to them, neglecting them, and cursing all the time. I continue to attend the Bible study, where Amanda has shown me love and is devoted to helping me know the Lord. Though I still struggle with sin, as we all do, my faith in Him is growing. I am seeking Him and awaiting more miracles.

I give thanks for what He has done in my life. It is Jesus who healed me.

"See now that I alone am He; there is no god but Me."
Deuteronomy 32:39a (HCSB)

———

A testimony from Good Samaritan Ministries in Guanajuato, Mexico. Originally published from Good Samaritans Ministries, edited and published with permission.

4

Scandalous Love

Jay A. Barber, Jr.

It was in the early winter of 1983. I was headed south to California on business in our recently acquired, used Chevy custom van—you know, the kind with the captain chairs, the swing up table and, in the back, a bench seat that collapsed into a bed.

I was nearing Cottage Grove, Oregon when all of a sudden the alternator warning light began burning brightly. I had just noticed billboards along the highway advertising Uncle Buds Chevrolet Dealership. I still had a long trip ahead of me, so I decided to go there to have the alternator checked out.

As I turned over the keys to the manager, he invited me to sit down in the waiting room; it was going to be a while because others were in line before me. I didn't think about it at the time, but I had left my briefcase in the car. I could have been doing some work while I waited, but instead I picked up a magazine left on the table for the customers to read. Little did I know how important reading that magazine would be.

One week later, it was a dark and cold December night, and I was heading back north to Portland, anxious to be home to my wife and family. Ice and snow lined the roadside and snow flurries were about.

I drove through Weed, California and was just beyond the final I-5 onramp of the town when I saw two figures standing on the on-ramp. One of them had their thumb out as I passed by. They were wrapped in a blanket that was shielding them from the ice and snow.

Now I had made a policy with myself that I would never pick up hitchhikers. But to my own amazement, I found myself slamming on the brakes and pulling to the side of the freeway. I saw the two figures, who I assumed were a man and a woman, running toward me through the flurries in my rearview mirror. I was at least a hundred yards down the freeway, so I started backing up to meet them. When they got near, I stopped and turned on the overhead light, and then stepped outside into the freezing wind, walked around the car and slid the old van door open.

As they arrived at the van, I got the surprise of my life—it was not a man and a woman, but two men wrapped up in the blanket. One of them suddenly thrust a small bundle from their arms into mine. I looked down at the bundle in the overhead light and saw a small child— a little girl. As I looked into her angelic face, terror struck my heart: her face was blue. Without thinking about it, I cried: "This child is dead! This child is dead!"

One of the two men began to cry and scream hysterically. They then climbed into my van and I began to shout orders to the man who was crying.

"Get her cold and wet clothing off," I shouted. "You!" I said to the other, "take off your upper clothing—your coat, your shirt—get down to your bare skin and get her body next to yours. There's a bed in the back. I'll head for the hospital!" I didn't realize it at the time, but that was the last freeway exit for the next many miles. It looked hopeless.

"Oh God," I prayed, "save that precious little girl." As I sped down the freeway, praying every mile of the way, I began to hear the most beautiful sound in the world: whimpering. Pretty soon, she began to scream and cry with full gusto. She was alive. She was going to be okay.

As we traveled north, I discovered that the father and his friend lived in Corvallis, Oregon. The young father of the little girl had only recently discovered that he was indeed the father of the child, but also had received the news the mother of the child was going to prison. Unless he came to Texas to claim his parental rights and responsibilities, the child would be placed in long-term foster care. When he got this news, he and his buddy decided to hitchhike all the way to Texas and get the child, and then hitchhike back to Corvallis where he would care for her.

I often think about and pray for this little girl, who would now be nearly 32 years old, wondering what she has done with her life. I especially think about her at Christmas time, not just because the story of Christmas is also about a small child on a cold and blustery night, but because in many ways the little girl with the blue face, in the late stages of hypothermia, represents you and me.

Like the little girl, we were without hope—we were "dead in our trespasses and sins"—until Jesus, the Son of God, came to save us. Through His Son, God took us into His scandalous love. He rescued us into the warmth of His arms. He knew exactly what we needed to be saved.

And God knew exactly what that little girl needed to live, too. The magazine I read in the waiting room at Uncle Bud's Chevy Dealership was all about what one needs to know and do to treat hypothermia.

"Put your hope in the Lord, for with the Lord is unfailing love and with Him is full redemption."
Psalm 130:7

———

Jay A. Barber, Jr. is President Emeritus of Warner Pacific College, Portland, Oregon.

5

Ugly Soup in a Pickle Jar
Susan Guenther

It was only a matter of time. Scott, my neighbor, and a wonderful husband and father, had stopped responding to the treatment for brain cancer.

Besides praying for Scott and his family every time they came to mind, I decided the most practical thing I could do to show them love would be to anonymously deliver meals to their front doorstep in disposable containers. That way, they wouldn't have to invite me in to visit, nor worry about returning my dishes.

Over the next several months, I covered their doorstep with homemade pies, cookies, soups, breads, and freezer jams—anything I thought might taste good to Scott and his family. However, as we heard reports of the cancer progressing, it became more and more challenging to figure out what foods might be appealing to Scott as his condition was declining.

One afternoon, as I was wracking my brains for something that might taste good to Scott, my immediate thought was split pea soup. I got busy assembling the ingredients, but suddenly paused when I realized that I only had yellow split peas. *Yellow split peas taste pretty much the same as green split peas,* I thought. So I continued whipping up the soup.

Yet when it was finished, it was ugly. Tasted good, but *really* ugly. I decided to put the ugly-looking soup into a cleaned glass pickle jar I had been planning to recycle. When I poured the soup into the pickle jar, it looked even more unattractive. Again, hoping to spruce up the looks of it a bit, I tied raffia-ribbon around the lid and tucked in a small wild rose. But it was not an improvement in my mind.

I looked at the clock. It was after 6 p.m.

Too late for a thoughtful dinner drop-off, I thought to myself, feeling like I had wasted time making ugly soup that I didn't even have the nerve to drop off due to the lateness of the hour and its "homely" appearance.

"Thanks for the great inspiration," I mumbled to God in a sarcastic tone of voice. I shoved the soup into the fridge, feeling like a lousy neighbor and bratty child of God.

The next day, however, I strongly felt God tell me to give the ugly soup to Scott. So I walked over to their house and dropped it off at the front door with some bread and jam, hoping to make a mad dash and not be seen. But as God would have it, a family-friend of theirs was leaving through the front door just as I was dropping off my "gift."

Scott's wife saw me through the open door and invited me to bring the food into the kitchen. She seemed overwhelmed, sad, angry and frustrated—everything I would imagine feeling if my husband were dying of cancer. As I loaded the items onto her counter, she eyed the ugly soup in the pickle jar with raised eyebrows as if to say, *what on earth is that?* I was immediately embarrassed.

"This is yellow split pea soup," I said, and then rambled on, apologizing for how ugly it looked in a pickle jar.

But I didn't get far into my apology, because as soon as I said "yellow split pea soup," Scott's wife broke down in tears and asked, "How did you know?"

How did I know what? I thought. She had to gather herself and gulp back sobs before she could tell me the story. Earlier that morning, Scott had told her that the only thing that sounded good to him to eat was split pea soup. But she'd angrily replied that with all the friends and family coming and going to visit, chat and pray with him to cheer him up, she simply did not have time to make him soup. Later she felt badly for snapping at him, especially since he had hardly ever asked for such specific items.

"God knew you were going to make it and bring it just in time for when Scott wanted it," she said.

Then I tearfully explained that I had made it the night before, but I didn't bring it because it was too late for dinner and I was too embarrassed over its appearance.

"You brought it at the perfect time—and it's beautiful," she replied.

A few weeks later, I attended Scott's memorial service. Just before the service started, Scott's wife grabbed me and proudly introduced me to the pastor and Scott's dad as "The split pea soup lady." Both men smiled and hugged me, thanking me for being a generous and supportive neighbor.

I have since learned not to question God when He gives me a specific task to do. Even when it feels inadequate, unimportant or mundane, God often uses the simple, humble and ordinary things to bless others. We should not deny someone a blessing because we feel our gift is unworthy. God makes all of our offerings acceptable and pleasing when given with a right heart, whether they seem ugly—as ugly as yellow split pea soup in a pickle jar—or not.

"Each of you should give what you have decided in your heart to give, not reluctantly or under compulsion, for God loves a cheerful giver."
2 Corinthians 9:7

———

6

Demons? Demons!
Larry Poland

One year, I was asked to be a speaker for a church's youth retreat near Orlando, Florida. I arrived at the camp on a Friday afternoon and saw that there were about 120 teenagers attending. After dinner, they gathered in a rustic lodge to hear my first talk.

Interestingly enough, I had chosen to begin talking about the occult and the phenomenon of demon influence and possession. Then I planned to transition into the concept of surrendering to Jesus Christ and allowing His Spirit to influence and "possess" us to produce the power and character of Christ in our lives.

Now I have spoken publically thousands of times on five continents for audiences as large as 20,000 people. I typically have no difficulty connecting words and thoughts. However, this Friday night was different. I could not keep my thoughts straight. The words wouldn't come.

And when I finally thought I was gaining traction with my young audience, one kid had a coughing fit, which totally distracted the group. Again, at a key point toward the end of the talk, another kid knocked a soda bottle off the bench and sent it smashing onto the concrete floor, again distracting my audience and me. I knew the talk was a disaster.

Walking away from the lodge after the session, I was met by two young girls.

"It's really interesting that you were talking about the occult tonight," they said. "There was this new girl, Laurie, on the bus ride up here who was telling us our fortunes. She was awesome! She told us stuff she could never have known about us."

All kinds of alarm bells went off in my mind. I know that demons are real. Jesus cast them out of possessed individuals, and I had had some encounters with them myself. That night, I prayed for God's guidance. The next morning after breakfast, I called the camp leaders and counselors together for a brief meeting.

"Something cultic is going on in this camp, and I think we need to be prepared and deal with it."

I told them about my struggle to speak, the strange and well-timed distractions, and the fortunetelling teen on the bus. I called them to spend some time making sure they were free of unconfessed sin, and then led them in prayers to claim victory and bind any evil spirits in the name of Jesus.

My next two talks flowed like water; there were no hesitations or distractions and I felt complete fluency and freedom in my spirit. After the evening talk, the two girls who had told me of Laurie the night before fell into step with me on the way to the campfire service. Laurie was with them, and they introduced her.

"I hear you tell fortunes," I said.

"Yes, I come from three generations of fortune tellers," Laurie shared.

"What do you think about what I have been saying about being filled with the Spirit of Christ? Does that make any sense to you?"

"Yes, it does."

"Would you like to pray and invite Jesus Christ into your life to forgive your sins and fill you with His presence and power?"

"Yes," she said.

"Then, pray with me phrase by phrase as I lead you. Dear Lord Jesus..." I started, but Laurie did not speak.

Again, I said, "Dear Lord Jesus..."

But again there was silence. I opened my eyes and saw Laurie convulsing. Her body was shaking and trembling from head to foot in the most violent of contortions and erratic movements. Instantly, I commanded: "In the name of Jesus, let this girl go!" Laurie went limp. I thought she might fall to the ground.

I started the prayer a third time, "Dear Lord Jesus..." Laurie repeated after me the entire prayer with a weak but earnest voice. She was instantly delivered.

Throughout that night, I was awakened three times with an urgent sense to pray for Laurie. I got out of bed and onto my knees and prayed until I felt her battle was over.

I saw Laurie the next morning at breakfast and pulled her aside.

"Did you have a struggle in the night?" I asked. She assured me that she did—multiple times. I told her that it would be crucial that she publically renounce her demon informers (she told me she knew their names) and openly profess her allegiance to Jesus Christ. She did so that afternoon in a sharing time with the entire camp. This sealed her freedom from bondage to the occult.

A miracle of divine power over the demonic world had occurred. There was no fancy exorcism and no complicated ecclesiastical ritual. It was simply the deployment of the supernatural power of the risen Jesus Christ through prayer.

"Jesus called His twelve disciples together and gave them authority to cast out evil spirits and to heal every kind of disease and illness."
Matthew 10:1 (NLT)

———

Larry Poland is the founder and chairman of Mastermedia International and founder of the National Media Prayer Breakfast. For three decades, his organization has provided counsel on the faith community to leaders in film and television. www.mastermediaintl.org.

7

No Weapon
Antoine McCoy

The tornado-warning sirens were blasting as I approached the road that led to the school where I teach in Harvest, a small city in Madison County, Alabama. When I entered the building, all the children were on their knees, facing the wall, and holding their hands above their head. This was the tornado drill position, as we had regularly practiced over and over again during the school year. *Just another practice, right?* I thought. I was not surprised or concerned in the least.

Yet as two more hours crept by, the sirens went off three more times. The decision was made to follow tornado drill procedures and bus the children home.

Two more hours later and still unconcerned, I was finally cleared to leave. During the 45-minute drive home across the county, the sun was shining again and the roads were peaceful and practically empty. Sub-divisions were intact, the local gas station had a few cars pumping gas, and people were at the local Piggly Wiggly buying supplies for this "severe thunderstorm."

What a waste of gas, I thought to myself, *to drive across the county and back home just for a severe thunderstorm and tornado warning. I'm from New York City. I've been in snowstorms and blizzards. They just need to lighten up down here in the South.*

Upon arriving home, I found that the power was out. Yet again I was not concerned—it was broad daylight. My wife Melissa was also home early from work and peacefully taking a nap.

It wasn't until I turned on my battery-powered MP3 player to listen to the local radio station that I first felt a stab of fear. According to the reports, a tornado had just touched down in a neighboring county and was heading toward Madison.

Melissa was eight months pregnant with our first child, and was noticeably shaken up as she held her belly and looked to me for comfort and direction. While I did not feel prepared to protect them, I immediately found a flashlight, blankets and pillows and placed them in an empty closet. This was the safest place that I could think of under which we could take immediate cover.

The radio was now reporting that the tornado had entered Madison County and that it would be in Harvest in a few minutes.

"Find shelter," said the speaker. This storm was real.

I do not know what prompted me to do what I did next, but I did what one is never supposed to do in the face of an impending tornado and thunderstorm—I went to the front door and looked outside. The clouds were becoming gray and overcast, but strangely, the air was still quiet and calm.

It was my wife who broke the silence. "Do you hear that?" she asked.

I strained to listen, but heard nothing.

"Do you hear that sound?" she asked. Again, I tried to focus my attention. Then I heard it.

"It sounds like a train," I said.

She immediately pulled me inside and said: "That's a tornado on the ground coming our way."

We ran to the shelter of our closet. I may have been unprepared and surprised in every other way, but now I knew there was a weapon that was stronger than any preparation or foreknowledge I could have had. Without hesitation, I grabbed my wife's hand and began to pray with all that was within me.

"Lord, please protect Melissa, the baby, and me. Protect our neighbors and our neighborhood from the storm. You are God of the universe. You have the power to lift tornados over our house and neighborhood. You promised in Isaiah 54:17 that no weapon formed against us would prosper and in Psalm 91:11-12 that you would command your angels to guard us in all our ways. Send your angels now and protect us. In Jesus' name, Amen."

With that short prayer, I held my wife's hand tightly and tried to comfort her. Now we were to wait. The wind was roaring and our house began to shake and rock lightly back and forth. While I was feeling absolutely horrified, I continued repeating these verses under my breath and praying that the windows of our house would not break, as the violent wind alone could cause major damage and great danger to us.

Five minutes later, it was all over. The tornado had passed and everything was calm. Melissa and I crawled out of the closet and thanked God together for protecting us and our home.

Fifteen minutes later, our neighbor from across the road knocked on our door and asked how we were doing. I told him we were shaken up, but thankfully no one was hurt. I saw that my yard had a few broken branches and some debris in it, but the damage was nothing compared to what the meteorologists on the radio had told us to expect.

My neighbor, however, was trembling. When I asked him what was wrong, he pulled out his smartphone and started showing me pictures. What I saw made my stomach drop. The Piggly Wiggly and gas station that I had driven by less than an hour ago was completely demolished. The houses in the sub-division only a half-mile away were totally destroyed. Homes in the neighborhood next to ours were in shambles and trees were strewn everywhere.

Yet our home and the houses in our sub-division and neighborhood were standing without any substantial damage.

Melissa and I were speechless. God answered our prayers for protection not only for our own home, but also for our entire neighborhood. In the aftermath of the tornado outbreak, we learned that the tornados that had swept through our area were some of the deadliest ever recorded in the history of the United States. They were classified as EF5 tornados, the highest-ranking possible for these kinds of twisters, and they had touched down that day in Madison County!

I cannot tell all of this tragic time, but I do know this to be true: one small, quick prayer of faith is a powerful weapon because we pray to a powerful God. Though we were unprepared, out of His own goodness and sovereignty, God more than protected us when we called upon His name.

"No weapon that is formed against you will prosper."
Isaiah 54:17 (NASV)

———

Antoine McCoy is a National Board Certified K-12 teacher who is passionate about helping adults and kids discover their God-given passions. You can learn more about Antoine, and can contact him, at http://antoinemccoy.com.

8

Anna's Answer
David Sanford

A question and mystery that has been debated for centuries is, "Does God speak to us today?" Two of my beloved mentors have insisted for 35 years that the Lord doesn't speak to anyone—*ever*. Sure, God spoke in ancient times to biblical prophets, but He stopped before the close of the first century A.D.

But I remember the first time the Lord spoke to me. It was at the end of an intensive time of prayer—quiet, yet crystal clear. I didn't know what to do, so I grabbed a pen and recorded in detail what He told me. Since that experience, my struggle has not been with whether God *does* speak today; my struggle has been with the thousands of times He chooses not to say a word.

This struggle was certainly true in the early days of the Great Recession. My wife and I were still recovering from steep business losses. Clients had canceled huge projects mid-stream, and then refused to honor contractual terms. In short, we were left with zero income.

At the same time our eldest son, Jonathan, was to be married in San Luis Obispo, California—900 miles away from our home.

My wife, Renée, and I did the math. It would cost at least $1,800 for the four of us—Renée, our son Benjamin, our daughter Anna, and me—to travel to the wedding, pay for the rehearsal dinner, and then travel home. But it didn't even look like we had the money to show up. As a husband and father, I cannot begin to tell you how helpless—and hopeless—I felt.

So the four of us agreed to pray for $2,000 "just in case" and, as always, coveted to tell no one of our situation but God. Within a week, we received an anonymous gift for $1,000. Renée, Benjamin, and Anna were thrilled. I felt smaller than ever. *Sure, we could get to the wedding, and pay for part of the rehearsal dinner, but what then?* I was depressed beyond words.

Sensing my downcast composure, my 10-year-old daughter tried to cheer me up. "Hey Dad, do you think that $1,000 came because *you* were praying? No, it was me! Don't worry about anything. God is going to provide." She paused. I didn't smile.

"In fact," Anna continued, "I want you to make a deal with me. You don't pray. Just me. And you don't get the mail either. Only I can get it. Promise?"

I didn't respond.

"Promise?"

"Okay." I turned to hide the grief and anger now racing toward my chin. Our trip was slated to start the following Wednesday morning. *What kind of father can't afford to go to his oldest son's wedding?*

The next afternoon, Anna came running through the door and said: "Dad, guess what? The check didn't come in the mail today. That means it *has* to come tomorrow, Saturday, Monday, or Tuesday. Isn't that exciting, Dad?"

"Anna, darling, another check isn't coming," I said. "I don't know why, but God sent only $1,000. That's all we're getting."

Anna smiled. "That's why you're not praying and not getting the mail, Dad!"

After school the next day, Anna came skipping into the house with the mail. She was almost giddy. "Dad, you're not going to believe it! The check didn't come in the mail today. That means it *has* to come tomorrow, Monday, or Tuesday. Can you believe it?"

No, I can't believe I'm in this situation, I thought. *I can't believe I can't afford to go to my own son's wedding.* I felt worse than ever.

Saturday was terrible. When the mailman came, Anna rushed out of the sliding glass door, over to the gate, and up to his truck. He handed her our mail for the day. Anna was bobbing up and down when she came back into the house. I'd rarely seen her so excited. "Dad, I can't believe it! The check didn't come in the mail today. That means it *has* to come Monday or Tuesday." She couldn't contain her enthusiasm. I couldn't contain my anguish, so I quickly turned and walked away.

How can I get her to understand? I wondered. *God doesn't always give us what we think we need. Even here in America, Christians often go through much worse things than this. Still, I'm so embarrassed, so ashamed. I'm such a failure.*

I didn't have a good morning at church. I felt completely dry, empty and hollow. I knew this feeling from one of my worst moments mountain climbing. I was hanging by one hand onto the edge of a precipice with no rope and more than 400 feet of air between me and the ground below.

I honestly couldn't pray. *Why even try?* I thought.

After school on Monday, Anna ran through the front door almost yelling. "Dad, this is so exciting! The check didn't come in the mail today. That means it *has* to come tomorrow!" She was literally jumping up and down.

"Anna, you don't understand. I don't know what we're going to do, but no check is coming. We already got $1,000. That's it."

Anna just smiled. "I told you. It's not your prayers. It's mine."

Sure enough, Tuesday afternoon Anna ran into the house, jumping higher than ever. "Dad," she practically yelled, "this is so exciting! The check *didn't* come in the mail. That means someone is going to knock on our front door in five minutes and hand it to us."

"That's never going to happen," I snapped, in the harshest of tones.

"But God told me."

"God didn't tell you that!" I yelled. I was so furious. I couldn't bear the inescapable shame that lied ahead of me.

A few minutes later, when I had started to cool off, I heard the doorbell. I yelled again (but more politely) for Anna to take care of it. Thirty seconds later she flew into the kitchen with the biggest brown eyes possible. In her hands she held an envelope.

"Pastor Jim just came to our door. He can't say who, but somebody came by his office and said, 'God impressed upon me that David and

Renée Sanford's family needs help. I feel it's urgent. You'll see they get this within the hour, won't you?'"

I couldn't hold back the tears. "I am so sorry, Anna. I said terrible things. I said God didn't speak to you. He really did. Will you forgive me?"

I'll never forget how hard she hugged me. After a minute she whispered in my ear. "I told you it was my prayers." I laughed hard for the first time in weeks.

Then Anna handed me the check, signed by the senior pastor of Spring Mountain Bible Church in the amount of $1,000.

Later I thought about my oldest mentor who had recently gone to be with the Lord. Yes, we're all in for a lot of surprises when we get to heaven. He now knows, beyond question, that God can speak to anyone, anytime, and in such a crystal-clear way that there's no other option except to know that God speaks.

Thanks to His incredible sovereignty, providence, holiness, love and mystery, you and I can stop telling God what He can and cannot do.

"And my God will meet all your needs according to the riches of His glory in Christ Jesus."
Philippians 4:19

———

David Sanford serves on the leadership team at Corban University, www.corban.edu. His writings have been published everywhere from Focus on the Family to Forbes. His book and Bible projects have been published by Doubleday, InterVarsity Press, Thomas Nelson, Tyndale, and Zondervan. David has been married to his wife Renée for 31 years. They have five children, and eight grandchildren (including one in heaven). www.linkedin.com/in/drsanford.

9

Consider it Joy
Rhonda S.

W hen my two children were in elementary school, my prayers for them were simple.

I prayed for them to do well in school, to have fun, to stay safe, and to make and be good friends. As they grew up, however, my prayers gradually changed. When my son, the younger of the two, was a senior in high school, my prayers—in addition to the obvious prayer requests like God's direction for his future, teacher-student relationships, deep friendships, and preparation for college—were intermingled with prayers for deliverance from drugs, alcohol, and sometimes even the safety of his life.

I mistakenly assumed that prayers could be the same for all my children—what worked for one child would work for the other.

This precious boy of mine had always been very sweet and sensitive. He was the one who would enjoy "mommy time" by cuddling with me any chance he had. He appeared to have a different personality than his sibling, but that was how God was molding and shaping him. I actually thought he would be the easier of the two to discipline and raise.

What I did not know was that he had been smoking marijuana for over three years, that some of the friendships he had were compromising his safety, and that he had dabbled in other drugs. I guess the transformation began once he entered high school. He was a bright, funny, and very kind young man going into his freshman year. I believe it was this year that he began looking more for the approval of his peers and doing whatever it took to accomplish this. Unfortunately, as parents, we gave him way too many excuses as to the change in his behavior and attitude. With each passing year, our relationship drifted further and further apart.

As his senior year progressed and I realized graduation was approaching, I was certain the Lord would answer my prayers by having him attend a Christian college he had been accepted to. I believed he needed new friends, a new atmosphere, and a fresh start. However, his bad choices continued, and so it was with a very heavy heart that we decided he would attend a local state university.

It all came to a head two weeks before he was to leave for college. My husband and I did not realize just how hard the devil was attacking our entire family; we seemed to be falling apart as individuals and as a whole.

I can still hear the yelling and feel the sting of tears. We had made an agreement that he would not have any drug paraphernalia in our home. I had run out to do a couple errands and when I returned I could not believe how heavily our home smelled of marijuana. It was then I knew what needed to be done, and was heartbroken in having to do it. I asked him to leave our home per our signed agreement.

The next 30 minutes were horrific. He proceeded to call me every name in the book, to beat me down as an individual, as a mom, and as a Christian with his words. Everything he did was done to hurt and infuriate me.

I was much calmer than I thought I could be. With every stab to my heart, I grabbed for God's comfort. At one point I did have tears in my eyes, but I was not overly emotional. As he grabbed a backpack and headed for the door, the thought crossed my mind that I, seemingly for the first time, would not have any idea where he was going, who he would be with, or what he would be doing. I watched my son take his skateboard and ride down our driveway until he was out of sight. The heartbreak was almost unbearable. Even with all the questions whirling around in my head, in that very moment, I heard God's still small voice say, "I love him more than you do."

In that moment, I knew something had to change. I did not know exactly how, but that didn't matter: it was time for change. My prayer life and devotions were transformed. Instead of praying for my son's circumstances, I began praying for the way I would handle them. My life verse immediately became James 1:2-3, in that regardless of my situation and all the heartbreak it was causing, I agreed to *count it all joy* and wholeheartedly give my son back to God, no matter what that looked like.

It was a transformation towards knowing the peace of God, which truly does pass understanding. While there were still tears and times of sadness, they were fewer and farther between. I had hope for my own life and the life of my son.

He was gone seven days before returning home. Although his recreational life using drugs did not change, he was willing to conform to our new rules and go to college.

The next two years of college, he was getting high. But he functioned adequately in family settings when he needed to, acting somewhat appropriately during the holidays and when he was home to be in his sister's wedding. I continued to wholeheartedly pray for and believe in God's plan for his life.

During the summer between his sophomore and junior year of college, he was offered a job. We were so excited for him, and believed it would help him gain responsibility and maturity. Unfortunately, it turned out to be an environment filled with people who were also using drugs. We knew he had still been using his drug of choice—marijuana— but now he was beginning to dabble in others. Praying my son through each day became a normal way of life. It was out of my hands; only God Himself could take care of him now.

I did not think it could get worse than the first time he skateboarded out of our lives. I was wrong. The second time he left was the worst day of my entire life. The words that came out of my son's mouth literally broke my heart into pieces. Yet to my surprise, I was calm and controlled. I remember sensing it was the influence of the drugs talking, not my son. Before he left, God's still small voice again spoke to me and gently led me to share with him some very powerful words.

I told him that from that very second, all the filth that was vomited out of his mouth toward me was already forgiven. I told him there was nothing he could ever say or do that would change my unconditional love for him. I had no idea what the future held for us at that moment, but because of the words I was sharing, I knew God was in control and I was not.

And then, for the second time, I watched him leave our driveway once again, this time in a car. With this departure, I physically felt ill. I fell onto our driveway, sobbing uncontrollably and gasping for air. The pain in my heart was absolutely excruciating.

This time, he was gone for only a few days. When he returned, we made it very clear that since we had already been down this road, it would be quite different. The first difference was that he was required to meet with a man who had experience helping addicts. The second difference was that if he did not keep up with his end of the bargain, we would finally follow through with previous idle threats by providing no funding for college, cutting off any and all financial help, and asking him to move out of our home.

After approximately three months, our son became completely drug free. This was his choice and his timing. This is his story.

Before this trial, I was striving for a pain-free life; I clung to my family as if they were my own. I had yet to wholeheartedly give them to Jesus. Without this trial, I would not have known the constant communion of a God who is our faithful Father, who takes care of my children whenever and wherever they are, and who supplied me with everything I needed as a mother.

The change in our son has been so extreme that friends and family often make comments after spending time with him. He is once again respectful, helpful, and a joy to be around. He often offers information about his whereabouts and who he will be with. God has a hold of him and is working in and through him. I trust that He will never let go.

One day, nearing the end of his junior year in college, I drove up our driveway to the place where I had fallen on my face in anguish the second time he left our home. In that very moment, I received a text from him letting me know that he had just read an excerpt from a devotional book I sent him. He went on to explain how God had provided just what he needed through those words that day.

Pure joy.

"Consider it pure joy my brothers and sisters, whenever you face trials of many kinds, because you know that the testing of your faith produces perseverance."
James 1:2-3

———

10

Feast or Famine
Suzanne Frey

If you and I knew each other when I was in college, I would have probably been on a diet. I was *always* on a diet. I was not obese, but my roommate called me "thunder thighs" and I was definitely overweight. I remember many mornings waking up and looking for something to wear that could fit onto my chunky body, wishing it would be socially acceptable to wear my bathrobe all day.

If I wasn't on a diet, I was on a binge eating everything I had deprived myself of while I had been dieting. I would start the binge at Baskin-Robbins, ordering a brownie hot fudge sundae, then go onto the local donut shop for a large apple fritter and a chocolate glazed donut, and then head back home to make and consume a large batch of chocolate chip cookies. All of this took place within a few hours; I'd be so stuffed I could hardly walk. This feast or famine cycle was a very normal part of my life. It was the way I dealt with life. It was the way I handled feelings of loneliness, rejection, fear and anger. Anytime I felt sad or when something didn't work out the way I wanted it to, I went to food to comfort me.

Pascal, a French philosopher, said: "There is a God-shaped vacuum in the heart of every person, which cannot be filled by any created thing, but only by God, the Creator, made known through Jesus Christ."

Even though I was raised in a supportive family that went to church every Sunday, I always thought God was "way up there" and that I was "way down here," alone in my struggles. It wasn't until my freshman year of college that someone told me I could know God personally through Jesus Christ. He wanted to be my friend. I didn't have to feel like He was "way up there." He wanted to give me life now and every day, not just when I went to church. At 18 years old, I asked Him to be my Lord and Savior, to forgive and cleanse me from all the things I had done wrong and to make me a new person.

It wasn't like the next day I suddenly lost all desire for food, yet God began working in my heart and life. I started reading the Bible and understanding that God loved me unconditionally: fat or thin, on a diet or binge day; what I weighed on the scale was a much bigger issue to me than it was to Him. Yes, He cared and wanted me to have victory, but my overeating was an outward sign of something that was wrong on the inside. I did not feel good about who I was. If someone were to ask me to describe myself in three words, I would have said: "insecure, unimportant, inadequate." Only God was capable of changing my view of myself.

He began showing me in His Word that He loved me. I started to realize that because I was made in His image, I was beautiful and precious in His sight. Reading through the life of Jesus, I began to understand that God wanted to deliver me from this bondage.

But I still felt the pull of my old habits dragging me down. I would make promises to God, put myself on more diets and programs, and even vow to fast for as many days as I could, thinking if Jesus fasted 40 days, so could I—oh, and dropping several pounds while I was at it. But when my promises did not last, I felt I let God down.

I was desperate to be free. I longed to be normal and see food not as my purpose for living but as fuel to help me live life with purpose. I was a prisoner, and it seemed that the harder I tried to be good and eat well, the harder I fell back into binging and depression. I was depressed because I ate too much, and even more depressed because I had gained another two or three pounds when I did so. It was a crazy cycle. By the time I graduated from college, I was 40 pounds overweight.

I related to Paul's words in Romans 7:15-24: "I really don't understand myself, for I want to do what is right, but I don't do it. Instead I do what I hate...who will set me free from this life that is dominated by sin and death?"

The answer is in Romans 8: living according to the Spirit of Jesus. I slowly began to understand the same power that rose Jesus from the dead lives in me. Therefore, I can triumph.

I put two requests before God: *Help me relearn how to feed my stomach only when it is truly hungry and to stop eating when I am satisfied; and help me learn how to feed my heart with a living relationship with You.*

I began learning that my overwhelming passion for food was not caused by physical hunger, but was a temptation from the enemy trying to keep me idolizing it. So in those moments, I began going directly to God by opening my Bible and getting on my knees in prayer. The Lord began giving me a passion for His presence. I began experiencing the "fullness" of God, something I could truly delight in.

Food and eating is obviously not a bad thing. It is a great thing. Not only is it necessary to live, but also a gift from God to be enjoyed. However, it was my idol. God provides food to fuel our empty stomach, not our empty hearts.

It was God alone who answered my prayers. He changed me. It happened over time, however, through one small choice after another. He led me to realize that temptation was not worth saying "yes" to and gave me His power and strength to say no. My small choices became my new habits which became my new behavior. His Spirit released, healed, and made me whole. He filled the empty hole in my heart that I was stuffing with food. All that time I had been famished for God. When I began feasting on His Word and presence I experienced even more freedom.

After college, I lost 40 pounds, got to a healthy weight and began feeling confident in my body. I began making healthy choices and have continued to do so up to this day—nearly 30 years later. I am in no way perfect; I still sin, but by God's grace, I no longer have this struggle. I no longer binge and live in fear of putting myself on a diet tomorrow. God completely set me free of a life controlled by food.

This is more than just a weight-loss story. This is a story of how God took an overweight, insecure, and very average 18-year-old girl and made her into a new creation. He broke the chains the devil held me in and launched me to liberty. Satan wanted to destroy me, as John 10:10 reads: "The thief comes only to steal and kill and destroy." But Jesus says: "I have come that they may have life, and have it abundantly" (NASB). Satan wanted to lead me to a place of staying fat and sad. God's destiny for me was to be healthy and whole. He heard my years of crying for deliverance and today I am no longer in that prison. I am truly free.

"He said, 'My grace is all you need. My power works best in weakness.'
So now I am glad to boast about my weaknesses,
so that the power of Christ can work through me."
2 Corinthians 12:9 (NLT)

———

Suzanne Frey has been a business owner and manager for over 20 years. She is actively involved with Moms In Prayer, leading Bible studies, and Toastmasters International. Suzanne and her husband, Ron, live in Oregon and have three grown children.

11

Bullet Stopping Prayer
Jim Moyer

*B*rrring, brrring! The phone rang out at 1:14 a.m. Sunday morning. "Your son has been gravely injured," an unknown voice said on the line. "We need your medical insurance information before we can transport him to the hospital."

Our fun-loving son, Jay, had travelled to the high country in northern Arizona with some friends. My wife, Carol, and I did not have a good feeling about the trip or the friends he was going with— and neither did Jay. At the last minute, however, he decided to go. Our daughter was way ahead of us on this feeling, but I will share more about her later.

Jay and his friends heard a deer moving above their campground, so they went to have a look. Jay was carrying a 22-caliber handgun. Why his friend brought it along, we do not know. Whether they saw a deer or not, we do not know. What we do know is that Jay slipped and dropped the gun. And it fired.

Jay did not immediately realize that he had shot himself, but he did feel a shock go through his body. The slug entered his groin, missing the main artery by the narrowest of margins. If it had severed that artery, he would have bled out and died before he could have reached help.

The long bumpy ride out of the campsite to the main road was torturous. Upon reaching that road they realized they were a long way from anywhere. Fortunately, there was an emergency phone by the roadside from which they called for help.

When help came, they called us. That phone call at 1:14 a.m. was a frightening wake-up call. I gave them the medical insurance information and they told me they would transport Jay to the local rural hospital, 45 minutes away. No good thoughts were going through our heads. Once Jay was at the hospital, I contacted the emergency physician on my cell phone, asking for Jay to be transferred to Phoenix where I knew he would receive better care.

"We do not have time," the physician said. "We need to do a work-up and operate immediately, or we might lose him."

The two-and-a-half-hour drive into the mountains was a horrible ride fraught with terrible thoughts of losing our son. After a while, Carol said: "Please stop talking about it. I can't take anymore."

We arrived at the hospital just as they wheeled Jay out of the operating room. He was alive and would surely make it. The road back would be long, but it was a road back.

Once we knew Jay was going to be all right, we knew we had to call our daughter, Kimberley, and let her know what happened. At the time, she was on a mission trip in Scotland, and the team had very strict rules that parents were not to call unless it was a dire emergency. We found the phone number and placed a very nervous call to Scotland.

One of the counselors answered, and I briefly explained that we indeed had a family emergency. He called in Kimberley.

I will never forget her first words to me. Crying, she blurted out, "Is Jay dead?" I was shocked.

She related to me that earlier that week she had a feeling Jay was going to die, so she asked members of her team to be praying.

What a joyous report I could give to Jay's sister: "No, Kimberley, Jay is not dead. He is alive!"

"Dad," she replied, "it was our prayers and the hand of God that stayed the bullet."

"Behold, I am the LORD, the God of all flesh;
is anything too difficult for Me?"
Jeremiah 32:27 (NASB)

———

12

The Last Assignment
John Warton

M ine was not a "foxhole" conversion. In fact, it was just the opposite.

It was 1969. Our mission was to fly along the Vietnam-Cambodia southern border to watch for soldiers and materiel from the north entering through Cambodia. Our Huey (a kind of military helicopter) had two pilots, two gunners, and one mission commander—me. Two guns ships supported us below, and a troop transport was flying with us. Once we observed enemy activity, we would deploy our assets as needed. It was 1:00 a.m. and we had just refueled after our first two-hour patrol. We were ready to takeoff for another.

I flew this mission many times over the past couple of months, qualifying for the air medal. It was my final assignment of a year's duty in Vietnam; I already served four months at a regional headquarters, then another four months with a Special Forces advisory team fighting with two battalions of national soldiers, and now a border surveillance and combat support mission. My tour was remarkably safe, despite combat engagements and others being killed around me. I did not have many days left in my tour, and this was my last assignment. But in fact, I shouldn't have even been flying this night because I was due to leave in the morning for a week's R&R in Bangkok.

And yet, there I was, commanding another surveillance flight.

The first two hours were uneventful. At a high altitude, we had spotted some convoys near the Cambodian capital, Phnom Penn, turning east after completing the long drive south from Hanoi. It would be daylight before they reached the Vietnam border. Our fuel started running low, so we returned to our airfield base to refuel. As we lifted off, we realized something was mis-set in the cockpit during that stop and the Huey had insufficient power to sustain flight. At barely 100 feet above the ground, a blaring siren went off in the headphones my team was wearing. The Huey shuddered, and then began to wobble. We started to pitch back and forth, and then descend out of control. Instead of whirling at 6600 RPMs, the blades were spinning at only 5800 RPMs. At 5600 RPMs, the Huey stops flying.

I instantly realized the danger of our situation. We had just refueled and were carrying flares and explosives. Any minute now, we could explode in a gigantic ball of flames upon impact. As I realized I was about to die, I clutched the metal frame of my seat. In "fast forward" scenes, my entire life flashed through my mind: grade school, my dog, our house, prom, and my fiancée. And then I prayed, "Jesus, save me."

I am sure it was an inaudible prayer; I think it was the "groaning too deep to be uttered" of Romans 8. It was, however, a deep and sincere prayer directed to Jesus. I grew up attending a traditional church and had heard many passages in the Bible. But when I left for Vietnam, my fiancée's parents had urged me to read the Bible. I bought a paperback edition of the entire Bible that I could carry with me, and read it that entire year. It was wonderful; it filled me with comforting and encouraging words of truth, and broad perspectives that I had never entertained before—even in college. It also filled me with convicting words about some of my conduct and attitudes.

In this moment, almost instinctively, my heart cried out to Jesus: "Save me!" And immediately I saw Him. He was dressed in dazzling white robes, as He was in the Transfiguration, and yet seated as if on a tribunal, like Abraham Lincoln in his Washington, D.C. monument. And suddenly the Huey stabilized and hovered steadily, without vibration, just above the treetops.

After several seconds in this position, the pilots felt confident to continue and began an upward ascent away from the base. But we had not flown 15 seconds before the same blaring signal was ringing in the headphones. *Shuttering, vibrating, pitching, dropping.* This time, however, I sat calmly with my arms folded in my lap. No further prayer. No conscious trusting for rescue from the crash, yet no fear and no anxiety. Again, just above the trees, the pilots were able to stabilize the Huey. A few moments later, we landed. Everyone ran away from the aircraft and we did not return to the mission that night.

It was my last moment in a combat operation. I left for my R&R a few hours later, and then was off to headquarters with my gear for a return to the States: President Nixon's reduction in force meant an early return home for me.

In those final moments of combat in Vietnam, the God of the Bible revealed Himself to me. He was not just a figure of ancient history, much less of religious fable. He was very real. He was accessible at a heart's cry. He was aware of my situation and more than able to intervene.

I had not survived a year's tour in Vietnam because I was careful, smart, or even just lucky. No, it was God who protected me through it all. It seemed incredible that Jesus could stop a Huey from crashing, but I had just experienced that. What was even more perplexing was why He answered my prayer and saved me. I was in no way worthy of His intervention; I was not even a churchgoer, a particularly moral man, or in the least noble. *Why?*

Over the next few days, I poured through the Bible I had read the past year. Now, however, I knew it all was true: Jesus was real, and He had died when I had not. He had been raised from the dead, and I too was alive even though I should have died.

Then I found 1 Corinthians 15:3-4, "that Christ died for our sins in accordance with the Scriptures, that He was buried, that He was raised on the third day in accordance with the Scriptures."

That was why He died—for my sins! And He had returned to life as I had experienced Him that night as the Huey was falling through the air. Four days later I confessed to the Living Savior my sinful pride, arrogance, and lust—all of which I realized He already knew—and put my trust for forgiveness and cleansing in Him.

Ever since, I have been able to say, in more than one way, "Jesus saved me!"

"For what I received I passed on to you as of first importance: that Christ died for our sins according to the Scriptures, that He was buried, that He was raised on the third day according to the Scriptures."
1 Corinthians 15:3-4

———

John Warton served five years in the U.S. Army after college. Following language school and special warfare training, he was sent to Vietnam in 1969. After his tours of duty, John married and entered business in Chicago. He and his wife have four children who have given them 12 grandchildren.

13

Squeezed By A Lemon
Kimberly Moxley

I had a vision of my perfect car. It was not a spiritual vision where the heavens opened up and I heard the audible voice of God. Rather, it was the less-than-heavenly vision of my young, naïve, and college student self with some grand ideas about what car she should be driving.

I dreamed of an SUV. I had worked my way through college, riding the metro for three years to my bank job and paying out-of-pocket semester by semester. Now I was months away from graduating with a bachelor's degree—completely debt-free. My parents were 3,000 miles away, so I was on my own for this first car-buying experience.

I thought an SUV was a cute car. Plus, it was big, and my train of thought was, "the bigger, the safer." I took a friend along, and soon we found ourselves at a used car dealership called Metro Auto Wholesale.

They were all smiles as they led me to a lovely-looking purple Suzuki SUV with a fancy "S" on the hood. I couldn't even tell you the model, I just remember thinking it was perfect. Not waiting another second, I signed all the paperwork right there on the spot. I gave them $16,000 in credit and they gave me the keys.

"Isn't it great that you can just sign your name and drive away with something as nice as *this*?" I said to my friend as we drove away. But I could not shake the weird feeling of apprehension and warning.

Sure enough, the next morning I started the car and a big plume of black smoke came out of the tail pipe. After three more black plumes within an hour of just driving to and from the store, I decided to seek counsel. I talked to friend who told me to take it in for an oil change, and when I did, the news that came next made me sick.

"Um, ma'am," said the mechanic, "this car probably has 80,000 miles on it. I don't think the oil has ever been changed since it drove off the lot as a brand-new car."

He continued, "See this pink hue that is showing on my fingers? That shows the engine is full of corrosion. Whoever owned this car before you ran it into the ground. This is on its last legs."

I tried to take the car back. Needless to say, they wouldn't let me. They had just made about $16,000 off a lemon and they were gloating and quoting back to me the fine print of their paperwork that I missed in my over-zealous signing.

The reality of what I had just done came crashing in. I went back to my dorm room and wept in embarrassment and for the lack of wisdom on my part. Two days prior, I was debt-free. But this would take at least five years to pay off, at the end of which I would still need a car. It felt like one horrible decision, something I'd done of my own will, without seeking God's wisdom and counsel, and erased everything I'd accomplished. What a fool I had been!

To add to the stress of this poor financial choice, I had been working hard in my job, making high sales numbers and doing everything to the best of my ability, but had not received a raise in two years. I realized that I would now need another job to buy a second car. And even then, I wasn't sure if I would be approved for another loan to help me buy another car because my credit was new and still being established.

I remember not eating much that week. I began crying out to God, repenting for my foolishness and asking for forgiveness. I asked God to deliver me from my own naivety and to somehow, in His mighty wisdom, get me out of this mess. The car dealership knew exactly what they were doing when they sold me the SUV, and for the first time in my life, I truly felt as if I had encountered wickedness. But then I was reminded that God is bigger than any devious plans of wicked men.

Through my sorrow over my poor decision, God reminded me of the many little financial miracles He had done for me in the five years

I had been supporting myself. He had directed my steps before in this area and I felt Him challenging me to trust Him again.

The day I was finally able to lay this mistake at His feet and let go of the heartache, I got a call from Metro Auto Wholesale* telling me that the company they had hoped would finance me said they would no longer finance me -- because my credit was too new. Apparently, I needed to be making at least 25 cents more an hour before they would even consider financing me.

In other words, I needed to return my SUV.

"I'll bring it back today," I said, and hung up the phone. I was never so relieved. Then, it gets crazier. Exactly one week later, I received a $2-an-hour raise in my job. *One week later.*

I *knew* God had been protecting me.

Soon afterward, a friend introduced me to the son of a man who owned a major car dealership in Portland. I knew him because he came into my bank's branch on a daily basis to make the car dealership's deposits.

He found me a car that was previously owned by a grandma and grandpa, saying they only used it whenever they needed a second car, which wasn't very often. It only had 47,000 miles on it and it was six years old. It looked brand new. It wasn't the SUV I envisioned, but it was what God knew I needed. I am still driving it today, 10 years after this ordeal, and it is going strong. And best of all, I paid it off in 3 years.

"Keep your life free from love of money, and be content with what you have, for He has said, 'I will never leave you nor forsake you.' So we can confidently say, 'The Lord is my helper; I will not fear; what can man do to me?'"
Hebrews 13:5-6 (ESV)

———

*(Metro Auto Wholesale is no longer in business).

14

That Was God

Dayle Lum

God has given me much in my life, including my husband, Andy. He is a godly man, loving husband, and great dad to our four children. He was a successful doctor who also took good care of his health and practiced what he preached. On a bright Sunday morning in January 2012, Andy, Tommy, the youngest of our four children, and I drove to church singing: *"You give and take away, you give and take away. My heart will choose to say, 'Lord, Blessed be your name.'"*

After church, Andy mentioned to Tommy that he felt dizzy. A few minutes later, Andy fell. Tommy called to me from the kitchen saying something was wrong. Andy told me to take his blood pressure. Three times I took it; each time it was escalating. We rushed to the ER.

The next seven hours were the hardest in my life. The doctors took a CT scan of Andy's brain and they could tell he had suffered a cerebral hemorrhage, which is a kind of brain aneurysm. The next thing I knew, Andy was in surgery to stop the bleeding. We were not sure if he would survive.

And so began a string of miracles. Tommy and I called the family to come to the hospital in Portland. Joshua, our eldest, and his wife, drove in from Washington; Anna took the next flight out from San Diego; Sarah was miraculously able to leave her research in Belize and fly home. Many people in our church family and my Moms In Prayer group came to the hospital. By 9:30 p.m., there were about 40 of us in the surgical waiting room, praying for Andy. When Dr. V., the neurosurgeon, came out, he said that Andy had suffered a subarachnoid hemorrhage brain aneurysm. The bleeding had somehow stopped, and the doctor was unsure how. *That was God.*

Andy was in a drug-induced coma for the next three weeks to keep his body still while his brain was healing. During that time, there were numerous emergency prayer requests for Andy. His blood pressure, temperature, and cerebral pressures would reach into dangerous zones because the part of his brain, which regulates those things, was impaired.

Yet I could see our loving Heavenly Father watching the hearts of His children and hearing all our prayer requests for Andy. I saw Him saying, "yes, yes, yes," to each request. Time and again, after the prayer warriors prayed, Andy's blood pressure, temperature, and cerebral pressures came down to their normal limits.

The doctors frequently had to take Andy's blood to see how he was doing. One day, a tech couldn't find a vein after inserting the needle a couple of times. Prior to being in the hospital, Andy had great veins, but with all the poking he had to undergo during this time, it became increasingly hard to find good ones. When the tech left the room, I put out a text message prayer request that he would be able to find a good vein. When he returned, he immediately found a good vein and was successful in getting a good sample. *That was God.*

Toward the end of the three weeks, they took him off the drugs. Yet I was still in a daze myself. Everything in my life had turned upside down.

I asked God to help me on this journey. On Sunday, January 29, 2012 there was a double rainbow outside—just like the day Andy and I got married.

"God is true to His promises," I thought. "This looks to be a good start of the day."

And sure enough, at 8:03 a.m., Andy moved his right leg and right toes. I called the nurse and she witnessed it too. This was the first time Andy had moved. He was starting to wake up from the coma.

Now there are three things in life that Andy's always kept constant: his faith in Jesus Christ, his love for me, and his sense of humor. That night, when Sarah was saying good night to Andy, she kissed him and he puckered up for another kiss. When she said, "Mom will be here in the morning," he smiled.

Soon afterwards, a respiratory tech capped Andy's trach for a little while. The first thing Andy said to me when he woke up was "I love you." God knew I needed that. During our 27 years of marriage, Andy has said, "I love you" to me every day.

As Andy's vitals seemed to be getting stable, one of the resident doctors in the Progressive Care Unit suggested he be sent to a skilled nursing facility as his next step towards recovery. But I felt pressure from her to have Andy transferred and didn't feel peace about him leaving the PCU just yet.

"Oh, Lord," I prayed, "please give me wisdom. If it is not safe for Andy to leave the PCU, then please make a way for us to stay."

God oftentimes answers in ways we do not anticipate. The next day, Andy's lab test came back with a positive for C.diff, a contagious bacterial infection that patients sometimes get when they have been on a large quantity of antibiotics.

Consequently, Andy had to be in isolation for 14 days until the C.diff tested negative. After a few days, Andy's blood pressure began to rise so high that the PCU couldn't treat it anymore, so he had to be transferred back to the Intensive Care Unit where he could have a nicardipine drip.

It was back in the ICU where we took another angiogram, as it was not uncommon to have another aneurysm once one had erupted. We found a third aneurysm in Andy's brain. My feeling a lack of peace to transfer Andy to the nursing home two weeks earlier suddenly made sense: we wouldn't have found the aneurysm in time and Andy would have died. Once again, God had answered my prayers. Even though it was not in the way I had expected, *it was God.*

But this news of the third aneurysm hit me hard. The tests showed this aneurysm with a threat of rupturing on a main vessel that controlled the right leg. The risk of Andy having a stroke during the surgery was very high.

I was sitting in the ICU waiting room and asking God to not take Andy away from me yet, when I felt Him say: "I won't. There is still more work for you and Andy to do."

"Is that you, God?" I asked. "Are you talking to me?"

"Yes," He said. Then I looked up through the window and I saw a little patch of blue sky shining through the Portland gray clouds. I began to tear up. You see, I grew up in Hawaii, so seeing blue skies reminded me of home. When Andy and I moved to Portland, the winters were very dreary to me, so I asked God to let me see patches of blue sky throughout that winter. He did, reminding me of His love every time. So when God gave me that patch of blue sky in the ICU waiting room, it was like He gave me a hug and confirmed His presence guiding us through this trial.

As Andy went into his third surgery, we asked everyone we knew to pray that it would be successful with no stroke or complications. Later in the night, Andy opened both his eyes. The saints prayed; God answered.

We thought that was the last one. But a week later, another aneurysm was found in his brain on the part that controls the left side of his face and hands.

Dear Lord, I prayed, *Let this be the last one.*

Dr. V. operated on Andy to clip the aneurysm in the right side of his brain. There was also some blood behind the aneurysm, which Dr. V. took care of. Did the aneurysm start to bleed? Yes. Did God hold that aneurysm from rupturing? Yes. *That was God.*

After two long months of living in the hospital, we were finally able to go to a skilled nursing facility. We were told that 60 percent of brain aneurysms result in death, but by the time we left the hospital, Andy had miraculously survived four brain aneurysms, with two of them rupturing before we could have the surgery.

Although I had always believed in prayer, it is cemented in me now, knowing that my Heavenly Father indeed hears the pleas of His children—and answers. He still performs miracles, and there were just too many to count.

When Andy first fell down in the kitchen, I didn't even think to call 911. Later we were told that because we brought Andy in so quickly, his chances of survival dramatically increased. *That was God.*

After the first surgery, when the bleeding somehow stopped and the doctor was unsure how, *that was God.*

I learned later that the doctors did not expect Andy to even wake up. His neurosurgeon said he beat 99.9 percent of the odds. *That was God.*

I was very comfortable in my role as doctor's wife and just gliding through life. But like a rose bush that needed to be pruned, I needed to allow God to cut off my attitudes of pride and self-sufficiency. God gave me a renewed purpose in His overflowing grace to become a conduit of His grace and love. He showed me kindness so that I could learn to extend kindness. I began wanting to do more than I ever did before: more giving, more grace, and more love. *That was God.*

Two and a half years after the first brain aneurysm, Andy started walking with a cane. His speech became clear and he began having short-term and long-term memory. He began feeding himself and showering with supervision. He started playing with a computer keyboard. We began working with a vision therapist to regain his right eye's visual field. Andy works hard at all his therapies, but it is our God, our Lord Jesus Christ, who does the healing.

"But those who hope in the LORD will renew their strength. They will soar on wings like eagles; they will run and not grow weary, they will walk and not be faint."
Isaiah 40:31

———

Special thanks to—
Our Doctors: Dr. Vora, Dr. Riley, Dr. Faheeh, Dr. Beam, Dr. Degen and Dr. Tilson
Our Nurses: Rebecca, Erika, Peggy, Bruce, Adrian, Sarah, Sheritia, Evelyn, Eric, Tsering and Shan
Our Therapists: Michelle, Jeff, Lisa, Julie, Blaise, Hope, Vlad, Melissa, Andrew, Jamie and Susan
Our Caregivers: John and Sakinah
Our Dear Friends: Jon and Susan Guenther, David and Dawn Golobay, Rick and Barb Martin, Melvin and Lori Yamase, Lisa Kyukkyuk and Linda Chelsky

15

Breaking the Cycle
Mary Guess

I was born and raised in the small town of Brazil, Indiana. My father was in and out of prison for most of my childhood—for being the town thief. My mother, brother, sisters and I were living on welfare—with all the stigma attached to it.

My mother was an angry, violent, and confused woman; and it wasn't until later I found out that both she and my dad were victims of their parent's abuse. My mother told me that she loved me, but her actions did not speak love. If my siblings did something wrong, she blamed me. I was the eldest, after all. She beat me on a regular basis; I even got a lashing if I didn't move fast enough for her. I always wondered: *do other mothers treat their children this way?* So I often stayed away from home.

My mother would have me beg to the neighbors or to nearby family for food or money. I did not like begging, so at 10 years old—when most little girls should be playing with dolls—I started mowing yards, raking leaves, babysitting, and working two paper routes to buy necessities for my family. I grew up fast. However, countless times when we would be painfully hungry, a bag of groceries would miraculously appear on our doorstep. Even at 10 years old, I felt God had His hand on my life.

When I was a freshman in high school, my grandfather's stepson, a senior named Sean, asked me to the prom. I was not sure why he asked me; only the popular freshman girls got asked to go. No one had ever asked me on a date—small town, dad in prison, welfare kid—so this was a big deal, and strangely my mom let me go. Sean's sister, Kelly, took me to a beauty salon where the stylist put my long brown hair into an up-do and dressed me up in a beautiful sky blue formal gown. I felt like a princess. Thankfully it was a double date with Kelly and her boyfriend, because on the way home, Sean tried to rape me in the back seat of the car with Kelly and her boyfriend right there in the front. If Kelly had not stopped him by God's mercy, I would have been raped that night. I was scared to death. When I got home, I went right to bed and cried.

Traditionally, the day after prom, everyone went on a picnic. Sean showed up at my door to take me, but I refused to get out of bed. Even after I told my mom what had happened the night before, she insisted I go. She was concerned about Sean's feelings being hurt, that he would be embarrassed if I didn't go with him. But I determined not to move from my bed. As I lay there on my bed, my mom began to beat and beat me. She pulled my hair, trying to yank me from the bed. Yet somehow, she could not move me. All the while, Sean was waiting outside.

So much for loving me, Mom! I thought. Yet the beating didn't hurt as much as her calling me stupid, telling me that no one would ever love me, and not protecting me from a potentially terrible situation. I had had it. I was so hurt and angry that I promised myself I would leave home as soon as I could manage on my own, and that I would never get married and never have children.

One day, when I was spending time in prayer with the Lord, I asked Him: "Where were you when Sean was outside and my mom was beating me?"

"Mary, I was right there with you," I felt Him say. "I was holding you on the bed; that is why your mom could not move you. Your mother chose to be angry and violent because that is what she knew, but I chose to protect you from things far worse than her anger." And then I felt Him say to me: "Trust Me, Mary, and follow Me. I will take you on a journey of change, choices, and victory."

Two years later, as I was nearing my sixteenth birthday, my dad had served his time and came home to start working. One day, he came home from work and told me that a "nice young man" was coming over to take me on a date Friday night and that I should be ready to go at 6:00 p.m. Of course I made a point to refuse, but he wouldn't hear of it. Little did I know that God was working a miracle.

Before this, I had been praying for God to send someone to love me. At lunchtime in school, two friends and I would sit in the balcony, sometimes pointing out boys we would date. One day, I pointed to a boy and said: "If I was really desperate, I would go out with that guy."

I thought I was so funny. Well, the laugh was on me. It was that boy who showed up at my doorstep on Friday night. His name was Mike, and we soon began dating. While we were dating, my dad messed up again and was sent back to prison. I was sure that Mike would not want to date me anymore, and that his family would not approve. After I told Mike about my dad, his response was: "I am in love with you, Mary, not your family." *Does God answer prayer?* Absolutely! Of course now I know the source of that love was Jesus. And so began my journey of redemption.

Despite my promise to myself that I would never marry, Mike and I married two years later. And despite my promise to myself that I would never have children—and the doctors telling us that we would probably never be able to—we had four beautiful children: David, Mark, Michelle and Bethany. My relationship with the Lord continued to deepen and He helped me start raising my wonderful children.

I continued to have a cordial relationship with my mom. She had called on me many times for help and I knew the Lord wanted me to be respectful to her and care for her. But there was still a lot of hurt between us, and it wasn't until her father's funeral that I began to truly understand why.

At the funeral, my mom confessed to me that my grandfather had sexually molested her from the time she was three years old until she married my dad at the age of 18. I wanted to vomit. My heart broke for her and what she had been through because of him. It explained her anger.

But then, my mind went to a different place. She had left my sister and I in his care many times. *How could she have done that?* I screamed inside. Yet I could not remember a time when he ever harmed me; and if he had, the Lord erased it from my memory. Still, this was very difficult for me to forgive. I wanted my mom to tell me she was sorry for how she had treated me during my childhood. But instead, she looked at me and said that "she had done the best she could to raise me."

Ouch! That was hurtful. My heart was so broken.

Although my mother never apologized for her abuse, I learned that whether she asked for my forgiveness or not, forgiving her gave my heart permission to heal. I learned that although forgiving her did not make her actions right, it made me free of bearing the burden of them in my life. The Lord helped me to forgive my mother, and in the process, took away the hurt I felt over my childhood so I was able to move on in my journey.

I realized that I had suffered from abuse because my parents had suffered from abuse, and they suffered from abuse because *their* parents suffered from abuse. It was a cycle that needed to stop with my family and me. I pledged to be the opposite of my mom, both as a wife and mother to my children. I was very involved in my children's lives, loving every moment with them and loving them deeply. They all grew up thinking they were my favorite.

One day while I was driving, my daughter Bethany, a senior in high school at the time, sent me a text message. I pulled over to see that she had simply written, "I love you, Mom."

Bethany had said she loved me a thousand times. But in that moment, I felt God say to me, "Mary, the cycle has been broken!" I knew exactly what He was saying. I wept tears of joy and I praised the One who can heal all wounds.

Jesus did not promise us a painless life. But with God's help, you and I can choose to not pass on the generational abuses of those before us. With His redeeming love and power, we can have a journey of change, choices, and victory.

"Forget the former things; do not dwell on the past. See, I am doing a new thing! Now it springs up; do you not perceive it? I am mak-ing a way in the wilderness and streams in the wasteland."
Isaiah 43:19

———

16

Between a Rock and a Hard Place
Lee Sellick

It was a perfect summer day. Two buddies of mine, Steve and Kevin, and I were climbing the North Mountain from the saddle between the Middle and North Sisters in Central Oregon. We had just finished lunch and were beginning to climb in shale and large boulders. Steve started up the ridge first, I followed about 100 yards behind, and Kevin followed about the same distance behind me.

As I walked, the shale slid and I only gained half a step for each step taken. Desiring to save my energy, I decided instead to hike on the rocks just ahead of me. As I came to the first boulder, I kicked it to verify that it was firmly planted, when I determined it was, I proceeded to jump onto it. As my weight shifted forward, the 2,500 pound rock broke loose and began rolling—pitching me into the air backward downhill. I landed on my daypack in a fetal position, and then quickly looked uphill to see which direction to move to avoid the boulder's path. Too late! A coffee-table-sized boulder hit my ankle and pinned my left leg against another boulder. I frantically tried to jerk loose, but to no avail.

As I lay with my left leg pinned down, I swiftly realized I was about to die. Any moment now, the boulder would continue rolling over my legs, over my body, and then strike its deathblow—crushing me completely on its way down the mountain. This all seemed to occur in slow motion, as my mind processed information at the light speed.

I thought to myself, "This is really going to hurt!"

At that moment, I stuck my hand out between my legs to touch the boulder, just as it reached my rear, and in a loud voice yelled, "Get that rock off of me!" The rock stopped, and then rolled six inches to the right to free my leg.

"That's weird," I said aloud. I immediately did a summersault downhill, away from the rock that had just pinned me. Due to the steepness of the terrain, I landed on my feet facing uphill. I was bleeding badly, and I checked to see if my injury was life threatening. It was not. I reached down and applied pressure to stop the bleeding as Kevin arrived to assist me to a safe area. Steve arrived soon after. Steve was an amateur photographer, so he began snapping pictures. Kevin was a medical student, so he quickly assessed the damage. The boulder hit my ankle but didn't break it, and proceeded to crush the soft tissue, scraping skin off the tibia. Yet I didn't break a bone. There was a deep puncture wound flowing a stream of blood, but that was stoppable.

"Did you see what happened?" I asked.

"I heard the rock break loose and start rolling," said Kevin. "I looked and saw you flying through the air headfirst downhill, looking at the sky. And then you were out of sight. I heard you yell, and then nothing. So I rushed to see what had happened and found you just standing, looking down at your legs."

We radioed for help, and I was picked up by a Life Flight Huey and taken to St. Charles Hospital in Bend. I met with the ER doctor, who had experienced a very similar crushing injury to the soft tissue. He was concerned about me losing my leg due to excessive swelling. To illustrate, he revealed a scar on his shin, which when cut, had allowed weeping so that the swelling would not cut off circulation. His prognosis was that I would be laid up for a minimum of four to six weeks. I would have to stay in Bend, so that he could assess the danger of the swelling. If it got bad, he would cut my leg open.

I asked if he had heard that eating fresh pineapple could keep swelling down. He hadn't, so I shared that its enzymes could mitigate the risks of swelling and bruising injuries. The doctor was skeptical, so I told him I'd try it and let him know how I was doing the next day.

A friend in Bend picked me up, took me to buy a pineapple, and then hosted me for the night. I ate the entire pineapple that evening. The next day I did the same with another; the third day I repeated the performance. Each day when the doctor called, I announced that there was no swelling or bruising—none! He didn't believe me, but allowed me to return home to Portland. A week later, after a total of four pineapples and a lot of rest, I was able to start working again.

I see two miracles combined in this near disastrous event: first, is that the huge boulder didn't crush me because I called out to God; second, my quick recovery was comprised of one week, instead of four or more.

I consider this a "love tap" from God to test and build my faith in adversity. God wanted me to see Him as the God of the impossible. There is no way the boulder should have stopped rolling down the mountain. However, God had already positioned an angel at my head and waited for me to call out to Him for help. When I did, the angel reached out, stopped the stone, and freed my leg.

This experience has helped teach me not to fear (as much) when difficulties arise or circumstances seem bleak. I am more aware of what God may want me to do in His service. I know that God can and will intervene on my behalf while there is more that He has for me to accomplish on this earth. Indeed, nothing can touch us if God wills that we still have work for Him to do.

"He will call on Me, and I will answer him; I will be with him in trouble, I will deliver him and honor him."
Psalm 91:15

———

Lee Sellick and his wife have two grown children, and a daughter-in-law, and owns a home inspection business. He loves the outdoors; in fact, talking about the annual wilderness adventure race that he helped develop gets him wildly excited!

17

10:15
Jodi Carlson

I have insomnia. Not just last night or for the past two weeks. Not in the past two months or even in the past two years. All 36 years of my life, since birth, sleep has not come naturally for me. Bleak nights of anxiety and despair have been unwelcome companions of mine. Doctors' offices and every kind of medication have made up my life story. All of the medical professionals I ever visited were perplexed. Finally, when I was 22, I saw a sleep specialist. His diagnosis? *Primary idiopathic insomnia.*

"What does that mean?" I asked, eager to finally have a name for my nemesis.

"It means that there's no medical, psychological or environmental explanation for your insomnia," he said. "And it means you've had it since birth."

Gee, thanks, Captain Obvious.

The unfortunate thing about long-term insomnia is that it's not isolated to your nights. Rather, it impacts your entire being: your body, your spirit and, most importantly, your mind. Over time, with some added "umph" from my genes, came its dreaded brother and sister: anxiety and depression. These three have come to form a triangular beast in my life—one I'm not proud of, but that I have come to accept just as one must accept the color of her skin.

I could tell story after story of my countless prayers regarding sleep. I cried out to God to just let me sleep, only to lie awake hour after hour with ever increasing anxiety that tomorrow would be a horrible day and, of course, drowning in panic that something was deeply wrong with me. Misery, hopelessness, and isolation consumed me. It seemed as if God didn't care and no one would ever understand.

One month, I was on the verge of collapse and at risk of losing my job because I couldn't function. I'd been there before, and had in fact quit my dream job as a magazine editor when I was 24 years old and moved halfway across the country to live with my parents in order to get healthy and rebuild. Eight years later, I again had a job I loved and was blessed with a supportive community of believers around me.

But the vicious tri-beast—anxiety, depression, and insomnia—was consuming me. It was all I could do to get through the day and collapse on my bed again at night, only to be robbed one more time of the one thing that could restore me. My eyes were hollow. My heart was numb. I echoed my tiny prayers over and over again: "Help me, God. You're all I've got. Deliver me."

I had learned over the years from Job 13:15: "Though He slay me, yet will I hope in Him." My pain does not imply that God has weakness. He does not. Rather, my perspective is limited. I am merely a human confined to linear thought. I am not privy to God's perspective, so who am I to judge Him and put Him in a box labeled "mean"?

On this particular night, I reached for a book on my bedside stand. I was in the middle of "Hinds Feet on High Places," a beautiful allegory about Much Afraid (the character) and the different terrain the Shepherd would lead her through, teaching her lessons each step of the way. I also simultaneously reached for my iPod. Those two never went together before; I would either read or I would listen to relaxing music to try to get my mind off of the fact I was not sleeping. But on this night, I reached for both. It was about 10:15 p.m.

I opened my book and began to read. This particular section was about Much Afraid walking through a forest, observing the trees and listening to the birds. Then the strangest thing happened. I began to hear birds. It was a soft, beautiful chirping—a delicate melody of praise. I heard rushing water, just as Much Afraid walked along a streambed. I stopped. I looked up at my bedroom wall. *What was happening? Where was I?*

After a dazed moment, reality hit me. My iPod was on shuffle and the song that just so happened to play in the very moment I started the forest scene with Much Afraid was a "nature tune," a song of wildlife sounds, which I had downloaded from a CD labeled "Relax into Sleep."

Tears immediately welled up and overflowed. God cared about me so much so that He would put these two together in that moment to minister to my spirit and remind me of my hope in Him. It was completely beautiful and humbling. In the same way Much Afraid was learning how to trust her Shepherd, I was doing the same. He cared. He loved. He would see me through.

The next day, I was just as exhausted as I'd been every day the previous month, but I had hope deep within my soul. My mom called to check in on me, as she had been tracking with me in my misery.

"Did you fall asleep early the last night, say around 10:15?"

My forehead wrinkled. "Well, no," I replied. "But God spoke to me at that time as He never has before."

"What happened?" she asked. I told her the story and she began to weep.

"That was when I prayed out loud for the devil to get away from you," she said. "I prayed for God to wrap His two palms around your head, to calm your mind, to hold and comfort you."

I still do not understand all the suffering I have had to endure as a result of the insomnia-anxiety-depression beast in my life. But I do know the triune God with an intimacy I cannot explain. No matter what I go through, I know that I am His and that He will remain God, my Shepherd, and my forever Hope.

"Though He slay me, yet will I hope in Him."
Job 13:15

———

Jodi Carlson, whose birthday is actually 10/15 (the same time God answered her mom's prayer) is a freelance writer and editor living in the beautiful Pacific Northwest. She has written scripts for Luis Palau's radio broadcasts and her published works include magazine articles for "Brio," "Brio & Beyond," "Multnomah," "Bend Living," "Just Between Us," "World Vision," "Proclaim!" and *Who Do You Think You Are?,* a book for women seeking to know their identity in God. She has a passion for all things nature, art, and ice cream.

18

Impostors, Yet True
Bill MacLeod

A few years before the disintegration of the Iron Curtain and
Communism across Western Europe, I was an unmarried,
20-something-year-old who had just finished working with Luis Palau
on a citywide evangelistic campaign in northeast Scotland. I had just
started a hitchhiking trip across Europe, and Bible smuggling on the
side was not exactly in my plan.

But as I was hitchhiking, I met a seasoned worker of Christ who
was adept in this undertaking. He invited me to come with him to take
Hungarian Bibles into Hungary's capital city, Budapest. Despite being
informed that within the past few months other mission groups had
been imprisoned for what we were about to do, we carefully loaded
boxes of Bibles into the car's secret compartments and started toward
the Austrian-Hungarian border.

As we approached the Sopron, where the crossing would take
place, I opened my Bible. The Lord brought me to a verse that I had
never noticed before, 2 Corinthians 6:8, where the apostle Paul is giving a defense of his sacrifice in ministry, saying they are considered
"impostors, yet are true." I realized that to surreptitiously hide these
Bibles and risk carrying them across this border would require me to
be an impostor. And yet in this, I was being "true" to the call on my life:
the spread of the gospel.

Just before the border, we pulled the car over to pray for our safety
and deliverance. Then we drove up to the tall barbed wire fences where

uniformed, armed guards in turrets looked down on us. After they searched the inside of the car, the border guards carefully examined the outside, and then let us pass.

Once on our way, my friend lifted his finger to his lips as if to stop me from saying anything. Sure enough, just a little further ahead, we were halted again at another entry point. Between the two entry-points, listening devices were used to pick up conversations by unassuming travelers who were unfamiliar with the lengths at which the authorities were taking to determine their visitors' true intentions.

When we arrived in Budapest, we found the house church of these Hungarian believers who worshipped in secret and who would be receiving the Bibles. I met a man, who was about my age at the time, and had spent his entire four years of military duty in jail simply because he was an unashamed follower of Jesus. In the faces of these vibrant believers, I saw something that I lacked. Even with my access to Scripture, and freedom to worship and fellowship, I felt naked and that *they* were the ones magnificently clothed. They were impostors, yet true.

The time came for us to make the exchange of our precious cargo. We drove around in our car, and they followed us in theirs, looking for a concealed location in the dark. Finally, we chose a spot on the side of the road, about 100 yards away from a brightly lit factory. Everyone scurried with their heads down between the two cars to transfer the Bibles as quickly as possible. Suddenly, someone looked up and saw a guard from the factory approaching.

Our transaction was thrown into a chaotic halt. Doors and trunks were slammed and we quickly screeched down the road before the guard could reach us. My heart was pounding and I quickly learned that missionaries have to become good at improvising. We fervently prayed as we drove around looking for another site to do the exchange. Finally, we found a secluded, pitch-dark vacant lot on the side of a road further up into the hills. After looking it over, we made our move. The Bibles were safely and swiftly shuffled without incident. After a quick thank-you and farewell to our friends, we drove our separate ways into the night. We were impostors, yet true.

We drove back to the border with a greater sense of relief and peace than when we entered. But as the guard motioned for us to step out of the car so it could be examined, I glanced at the backseat. To my horror, I noticed I had left laying there the Celtic Bible I had brought with me from Scotland. The guard immediately picked it up and started looking through it.

The "mission-accomplished" feeling evaporated in an instant and the words in 2 Corinthian 6:8, which had been bringing me such conviction and hope, suddenly felt powerless—as did I. Inside, I cried out to the Lord. Lifting my head and eyes toward the distant Hungarian hills of Sopron, I immediately remembered the distinctly comforting words of Psalm 121:1-7: "I lift up my eyes to the hills. From where does my help come? My help comes from the Lord, who made heaven and earth...The Lord will keep you from all evil; He will keep your life. The Lord will keep your going out and your coming in from this time forth and forevermore." (ESV)

The guard could not read the language the Bible was written in, so he turned to me for an explanation. I remember mumbling something about it being "just a book." *Just a Book, indeed!* For a moment he hesitated, then he threw it back onto the seat and hastily motioned for us to leave.

No one had to sign for me to be quiet this time as we sped toward Vienna. We drove in silence for a few miles, taking in the care, protection, and wonder of God. It was a short journey, yet sufficient for the journey of a lifetime. God delivered us. We were impostors, yet true.

"...We are treated as impostors, and yet are true..."
2 Corinthians 6:8 (ESV)

———

Bill MacLeod has been a mission-mobilizer for over 30 years, dedicated to city-wide people movements while serving in an evangelistic organization, a national men's movement, and as a local church missions pastor. He currently serves as the founder and executive director of Mission ConneXion, a church-missions-mobilizing effort.

19

Unexpected, Beautiful Joy
Lily Crowder

I grew up knowing the Lord in a Christian home. Though it was a very broken, dysfunctional Christian home, I was raised with the knowledge of Christ. But I became your typical Christian-good-girl gone bad. After a series of sad events and foolish choices in my life, I turned away from my faith and was basically plain ol' naughty! The unwise choices I kept making, and the harmful people I kept migrating toward, left me in a state of depression and emptiness. I knew enough of what was right and godly, but I refused to live that way. I hated myself for it. My struggle with identity and feelings of unworthiness made me hungry for healthy affirmation and affection. I was your classic girl who was "looking for love in all the wrong places." It wasn't too long before I ended up pregnant at the age of 18.

I had to humbly face my old Christian community and small town friends, move in with my mom, and live off of welfare. It was such a lonely, humiliating time in my life. Being "knocked-up" and abandoned by someone who had claimed to "care for me" was overwhelmingly heartbreaking and humbling, to say the least.

For the duration of my pregnancy, I focused on trying to get my life back together. I had a desperate hunger and longing to make up for all the wrong I had done. I felt so undeserving of anything good. I thought I was going to be punished for all my sin and that God was going to give me a horribly challenging baby. I felt so alone, undeserving, unworthy, unfit, worthless and scared, so I asked God to turn the mess I had made into something beautiful.

When my labor finally came on, I had no idea what was about to take place. I could only anticipate an outcome from a place of fear, rejection, and uncertainty. But in that fragile place in labor, I could feel the love and gentleness of Jesus. That day changed my life forever.

I gave birth to a beautiful and healthy baby girl. She was amazing—such perfection, such a tiny wonder! In those first few moments with her, I couldn't help but thank and praise the Lord for her life. My love for her came from deep within, and was overwhelming and unexpected. I never knew that having love this deeply for another person existed. I named her Maile (My-lee, which is Hawaiian for "beautiful") Joy. Knowing I did not deserve this, I asked God: "What about my punishment? I did everything wrong, and yet here I am holding this beautiful, perfect baby girl—a perfect gift." Every day she got cuter. She had two huge dimples when she smiled and glorious, perfect baby rolls. She was so happy. To this day, I still call her "Smiley Maile."

As a new mom, I mostly felt God's grace and presence in the ways He provided a natural, new love and inspiration in me for Maile. When all my friends were out on the town, and I was home alone with my baby, I knew God had a plan and that Maile was one of the best parts of it. I really enjoyed being a mom, even a single mom. Maile and I did everything together. God also provided a job as a nanny where I was able to take her with me. Because of her wonderful demeanor, I was even able to take her to my college classes.

But at times, when I was still, I would think of her future and the lack of a father. I would feel guilty for all my inabilities to provide everything I thought she needed. Those feelings were paralyzing at times. Even still, I would talk to God about it. I asked Him to provide in His way and timing what we needed most.

The day after I turned 22, I met a literally "tall, dark, and handsome," and witty man named John. I could barely stand when I first spoke to him, nor could he. Something in me knew that he was the "one." Yet I was afraid, and later on even tried to hide from him in the basement of the church where we met. It was so obvious to everyone around us that there was a little more than chemistry between us. It was love, for the first time in my life, real supernatural love.

Along with meeting and falling in love with me, John also fell in love with my little blue-eyed girl. While we were engaged, and while John was away on a work trip, he wrote me a letter confessing what was taking place in his heart for my little girl. The idea of being her father was effortless and natural, like it had always been part of the plan.

John adopted Maile shortly after we were married. She was three at the time, and has grown to know and trust him like he had always been there from the very first day. Maile became, and still is to this day, daddy's girl. The bond and connection that they share is amazing to see. Since our marriage, God has blessed John and I with three more delightful children.

Before I met John, I remember a time when my daughter was about two. I was alone in my little home, and I opened my Bible for the first time in a long while. I found myself reading Luke 7:47: "Therefore, I tell you, her many sins have been forgiven—as her great love has shown. But whoever has been forgiven little loves little." I am so thankful that because I have been forgiven much, God has enabled me to not only love again, but to love much.

I still remember the feeling of being an outsider, as now, when I see a young girl or single mom who's struggling, I am able to encourage her by sharing my story. I truly wouldn't trade this transformation and what God has done for anything, even with all the awkward and hard moments involved. God's love unexpectedly burst into my life, and made things new.

"We love because He first loved us."
1 John 4:19

—————

Copyrighted material from *Grace for the Contemplative Parent*, by Lily Crowder, edited and used with permission.

20

Lost Coin
Lauren Frey

I like to take the time to pick up lost pennies. Of course a quarter, dime, or nickel is more exciting to find. But pennies? The useless "copper"? The ones that get kicked around until they stick to the ground on some chewed up piece of gum? Yes. I've found around a hundred of them so far. I keep them in a jar. I'm a dollar richer, now, thank you very much.

One day, I found more than a penny. Actually, it found me. Not on a sidewalk, but in a church while I was on a mission trip in my home state, Oregon, with a team from my California-based ministry school.

Our team of 15 really only had one mission: to flood the streets with "the evidence of things unseen"—with the supernatural, tangible *love of the Father.*

Tuesday morning, the fourth day our trip, I woke up and read Matthew 7:7: "Ask and you will receive, seek and you will find, knock and the door will be opened."

I felt God tell me that He was serious about that. He meant to give my team and I things we asked for by grace, in faith, and in His Name. He wanted the things of His kingdom to be *received, found,* and *opened.*

Lord, what does that look like? I prayed. *Teach me today.*

Later that day, the team was having a meeting in our host church's office. Before the meeting began, a team member, Jared, showed me a Bible verse that had struck him that morning. He was reading it from one translation, and I got curious as to what it read in another.

I walked over to the church's donated-Bibles shelf. A baby-pink Bible, spine all worn, caught my eye. When I sat back down on the couch and flipped it open, a crispy and perfectly folded $100 bill fell from the pages—who knows where it came from!

"Jared, look. This just fell out of this Bible."

"What?" he said, smiling, "are you serious?"

I held it up to the light. "It's real."

I took it to the pastor. "Um, Pastor Jim," I said, "this just fell from a spare Bible." I tried to give it to him.

"No, no," he said with a grin, pushing it back into my hand. "Keep it. I believe God has something for you to do with it."

As the meeting began, I tucked it away in my red wallet. *Okay, God. That was cool. Will you show me what You want to do with this?*

Two days later, in the middle of a rainy afternoon in downtown Portland, we had a two-hour timeslot to go out on the streets and pray for anyone the Lord led us to. I grabbed my purse, an umbrella, and a simple drawing of the word "freedom" with flying birds in the middle, which I had drawn the night before. Then I, along with two team members, Lindy and Michael, started walking toward the waterfront.

"Lord, lead us," we prayed out loud. "Show us who You want us to minister to today."

We'd walked two blocks when a woman caught our eye. And then we caught hers.

"Excuse me!" she cried to us. "Do you know where Pioneer Square is?"

"Are you new around here?" we asked.

"Yes," she said. Michael, who was familiar with the city, gave her directions to the Square. But as it seemed God had highlighted her to us, or us to her—however that had worked—we knew we were supposed to keep talking with her.

"What's your name?"

"Leah," she replied.

"What brought you to Portland?" Leah told us she had just been released from four years in prison. She also immediately confessed she had become a Christian and was basically homeless, in need of money, in need of a job, looking for a fresh start, and a church to fellowship in.

Lindy asked Leah if we could pray for her. She said "yes." As we started praying for her right there in the hustle-bustle of the streets, she started tearing up. The Holy Spirit's presence became so strong as we felt Him guiding our prayers and giving us specific words of encouragement for her. After a few minutes of praying, the Holy Spirit reminded me of the $100 bill in my wallet.

"Leah," I said. "I have something to give you."

I first gave her my umbrella, then the picture that said "freedom," and finally the $100 bill. When she received it, she started crying even more. It looked like God gave her a hug that nearly knocked her over.

"No way!" she finally said. "You won't believe this." Leah began telling us that that very morning, an old friend from her past life had contacted her, asking her to help with a drug deal. It would have been a $200 deal. She would have been paid half.

"But I refused to do it," she told us. "I told God, 'No, I am not going to do this. I believe You will provide for me.'"

And with that, we were speechless. "Leah, God *loves* you," we said.

"I know," she said, through tears, as if realizing it for the first time.

I'll never forget the beautiful smile beaming from her face as she realized her Heavenly Father heard her prayers, knew her heart, honored her faith and obedience, and had miraculously provided for her—all in one day. We prayed with her again and gave her some names of ministries and churches to plug into in the Portland area, including the church that was hosting us.

I know what it's like to search for pennies. But I admit, they are pretty worthless. This hunt doesn't do anything for me—except, I guess, it does give me joy to just *find things*.

If I find just a little joy in finding pennies, imagine the joy God feels when He finds, or rather reclaims something of true value, a child of His own. In Luke 15, He tells three parables of lost things being found: one of 100 sheep, one of 10 coins, and one of two sons. Jesus enjoys finding things, too. Lost things.

While I was absolutely blown away to witness God give Leah the unmerited grace of provision that day, I also felt an unmerited grace in my life to partner with Him in the process! I did not deserve to be the one to give her that $100 bill. I will never be worthy of giving what is God's—even *that* is by grace.

But God answered my prayer to teach me more about what it looks like to live out of the kingdom—a kingdom with endless storehouses of things to be readily *received, found, and opened.*

Most of all, He instilled in me a fresh hunger that day to live more aware of Him, the pursuing Father of all, who goes after the one and is ever seeking and saving that which was lost.

"There is joy in the presence of God's angels
when even one sinner repents."
Luke 15:10 (NLT)

21

Yahweh Rophe
Ferol Chew

It was a beautiful spring day when I waved my 15-year-old son, Aaron, a loving good-bye as he got on his moped to visit a friend. Little did I know that within the next 10 minutes our world would be shaken.

As Aaron approached the Rhododendron Garden, a van stopped in front of him, attempting to turn into its entrance. But Aaron didn't see it stop. He drove headlong into the back of the van, flying over the moped's handlebars, breaking both legs as he landed and knocking himself unconscious by suffering severe head trauma. Within minutes, he was rushed to the hospital where he went directly into surgery.

It wasn't until three hours later, as I was fixing dinner, that I received the news of the accident. The phone rang and it was one of Aaron's friends who had heard he crashed on the moped. I dropped everything as fear crushed my heart. After telling my husband, Larry, we started calling emergency rooms in the area. Thankfully, the second ER that picked up the phone informed us that they indeed had a victim who fit Aaron's description and that he was in surgery.

When Larry and I arrived at the hospital's ICU, a neurosurgeon informed us that only 50 percent of patients with these kinds of injuries live. There were no gentle words, no compassion, just brutal facts, and the worst kind a parent can possibly hear. He also told us that if Aaron survived, he would mentally never be the same.

Aaron was given multiple blood transfusions. A probe was inserted into his skull to relieve pressure and to watch for needed surgery. Both legs were set, including a very bad compound fracture of the left thigh, which was in traction. He had bruised kidneys. For five days, he remained unconscious in the ICU due to severe head injuries.

Now prayer is something we don't need to do on our own. During this time, our pastors, church family, friends, and Aaron's sister and grandparents never left our side. These prayer warriors didn't let us give up. Together we asked Yahweh-Rophe, which means The Lord Who Heals, for the sparing and healing of Aaron's broken body, keeping our focus on God's power to do so.

Life in the hospital was filled with fragile moments of not knowing how many days we would be there and what kind of news would end those days. One day I retreated by myself into a dark room.

With a breaking, fearful, and defeated heart, I cried out to God and gave my precious child up to him. Aaron had always been strong in his faith and loved God, but I prayed that if it were Aaron's time to go, that God would receive him. It was the hardest thing I had ever done, for although I had prayed and given him to God before, in this moment I gave his life over to God. I let go of him, rededicated him to God—I put the whole situation in God's hands.

He remained in ICU for 11 days, at the end of which Aaron's body began to heal. After 30 days, he was able to come home. After months of rehab and physical therapy, Aaron proved the doctors wrong.

During the last doctor's visit, the doctor confessed: "It was not medicine that healed your son."

Not only did Aaron live, but his mind and body were made completely normal and the accident in no way affected the way he walks or lives now—with the exception of him having some metal in the leg, which is only noticeable when he walks through the detectors at airport security. He's a finish carpenter and very active young man.

God heard our prayers when we cried out. He answered us as we depended on His mercy and power. It was up to us to trust God's sovereign ways of love. My job was, and is, to allow His Word to confront my fears and hold me in the deepest of valleys, as He lives in me and leads me on.

"Now faith is the substance of things hoped for,
the evidence of things not seen."
Hebrews 11:1 (NKJV)

———

22

The Bear

Bill Sundstrom

Spring break my freshman year in college, I was a young believer, and my friends, Dan and Buck, invited me to come along on a backpacking trip in the Porcupine Mountains of Northern Michigan. As three carefree young guys, we roamed and hiked around, sometimes talking to fellow travelers about the Lord. We didn't even have a tent—just a piece of plastic we rigged up as a lean-to tent for sleeping. But toward the end of our seven-day trip, we ran clean out of food.

"No problem," we said. "We'll just do a little fishing."

Far from a regular campground, we pitched our lean-to in a random spot near Lake Superior. Tossing our lines in a little stream that ran by our camp, we tried our luck. All we could catch were suckers—bony little fish generally considered inedible. But we were starving, so we cleaned and ate them anyway. After dinner, we carelessly tossed the bones into the woods near our campsite.

That night, as we were sitting around the campfire, we heard something big crashing around nearby.

"Squirrels?" I said, hopefully.

"No way," Buck replied, "too big."

In that moment, we all remembered the ranger's warning before we took off, "Watch out for bears!"

I thought of how exposed we were, with not even a real tent to hide in. Dan suggested we pray. In my young faith, I was not sure God could handle this, but it still sounded good to me!

Dan prayed and asked the Lord to send the bear somewhere else, as we were His servants and had been trying to trust Him and make Him known on this trip.

And then, we went to sleep under our lean-to tent and passed the night in peace.

The next morning, we found fresh bear droppings about a hundred yards down the trail. Then we learned that two couples a few hundred yards on the other side of us had cowered in their tents and watched a bear rip open their packs looking for food. Not only had he taken their food, but he had eaten 40 hits of speed as well!

And there we were, right between these two points. The bear must have walked—or floated—amid the trees and right through our camp-site to get from one point to the other. I was amazed that God really had answered our prayer.

Yet it seemed that the Lord wanted to drive the point home. An hour or so later, Buck went down to the shoreline of Lake Superior to collect driftwood for a fire. As he was about to toss it on the fire, Dan said: "Wait a minute! It looks like there are words on that piece of driftwood."

Dan grabbed the jagged section of the 2x4 inch board and cleaned the dirt off it. As the words emerged, we gasped. There on that weather-beaten piece of driftwood, somebody had carved the words: *God answers prayer.*

"God is our refuge and strength, an ever-present help in trouble."
Psalm 46:1

———

As a former writer and editor with Worldwide Challenge magazine, Bill Sundstrom has travelled the globe in pursuit of stories, visiting some 70 countries along the way. Whether telling about a villager in the Andes, a banker in London, or a bear in the woods, he gets at the heart of a story and brings distant places –and people – to life. Bill and his wife live in Pennsylvania, and have three children.

23

The Fourth Child
Dinah Schild Nicholson

I was lying on the sun-soaked wood floor of my childhood home staring at a photo in a magazine. *Thirteen children.* It was a photograph of Harry and Bertha Holt, of Holt International Children's Services, and their large family. I was five years old and the youngest of five children. I knew what it was like to be part of a big family, yet what held my attention the most was that eight of these children were Korean. They were *adopted.* And at that moment, God planted a seed in my heart for adoption.

My first plan was to plead with my parents to adopt a little sister or brother. I was unrelenting, yet all of my five-year-old charms were insufficient. Then the Holy Spirit whispered into my heart: "One day, you will adopt your own child."

I presumed He meant I would adopt if I were unable to give birth. Thirty-one years later, however, I was happily married to a supportive and loving husband, Steve, with whom I had three children in our first five years of marriage.

Steve and I were extremely busy with full time careers in the financial services business. In addition, we were in the throes of bringing our clients through the 1987 market crash. That year, to my astonishment, I heard God's voice whisper, "You shall have a fourth child." And I knew He meant that it was time to adopt.

My exhausted husband suggested we wait five years. In that time, God did not remove my passion to adopt. While volunteering for an adoption agency, we continued to pray and talk about it. We eventually named this dilemma, "The fourth child issue."

One day, I compared the reasons for buying a boat, which was my husband's dream, to adopting a fourth child. The pro's and con's were almost identical, except that it would be hard to hug a boat and one cannot water-ski behind a child.

We entered into counseling, hoping to convince my heart that adopting a fourth child would be "unwise" in our over-packed schedules. But after listening to us, God would have it that the counselors concluded we should adopt. God was a gentleman and He waited for our free-will decision. And now, years later, we often laugh about the moment when my husband retorted: "You didn't tell me that you wanted to adopt a child before we were married."

"If I had told you all of my dreams and passions," I had quickly replied, "you would have been afraid to marry me!"

In faith, we started the adoption process. After involving the entire family in the decision, we agreed to pursue adopting from a Russian orphanage. By the end of 1996, we had passed the home study, completed many forms, and jumped through the normal setbacks.

In January of the next year, we were shown the medical report of a healthy three-year-old girl named Galina Valentinovna Merzlyakova. She was born on Christmas Eve of 1993, which was a night I vividly remembered having a heartfelt talk with God about the "fourth child" calling.

After a slow train-ride all night through the Ural Mountains, we arrived in Serov, Russia on March 11, 1997. It was a cold and snowy morning. We stepped off the muggy train into the cool air.

As we reach the front door of the orphanage, we felt like Lucy in C.S. Lewis' *The Lion, Witch and Wardrobe,* walking through the back of the wardrobe and into a new season and territory.

Within an hour, our new daughter Galina Victoria Nicholson, or "Tori," was placed into our arms. She was tiny for a three year old, at only 23 pounds and 30 inches tall. She was shy, of course, but excited. We instantly won her over by blowing soap bubbles.

As we learned years later, Galina was born prematurely as the eleventh child of a very poor family. The Russian government had already removed three of the children from the family to an orphanage, and the maternity ward would not allow the birth mother to take Galina home. She spent the first three months of her life in the hospital and then was transferred to the orphanage in Serov.

Tori is now 20 years old. She is spunky, courageous, friendly, and trusting. Steve and I remind Tori that God always had a plan for her and that His hand is on her. We are thankful that her heart is with God and that she has conversations with Him. It has been one of the greatest pleasures of our lives to raise and love her.

To quote Bertha Holt, the woman who God used in my life at five years old: "All children are beautiful when they are loved."

"You received God's Spirit when He adopted you as His own children.
Now we call Him, 'Abba, Father'."
Romans 8:15b (NLT)

———

24

Beating Autism
Bernadette S.

Jacob, our eldest son, was only three years old when the words Autism, ADD, Sensory Integration Disorder, and Asperger's Syndrome became commonplace in our home.

The diagnosis of Jacob having all these issues helped explain why he did not act like other children: he was so sensitive that even wind physically hurt his skin. Oftentimes, a mowing lawnmower at the end of our street would send him into a frenzy and sudden laughter in our home would make him cry. And at church, the only way to keep him happy was to *be* the Sunday school teacher.

I knew Jacob would never be "normal," but I hoped he could learn how to overcome the challenges he faced. I knew God doesn't make any mistakes, so He didn't make one when He made Jacob.

I prayed God would prove Himself faithful to Jacob, helping him with every difficult circumstance he faced and giving him His peace in our loud and busy world. I prayed Jacob would be able to live a normal and productive life, learning how to channel his gifts for God's glory. I wanted Jacob to live certain that God made him with a "plan and purpose."

Although my husband and I had planned for me to work a teaching job throughout parenthood, doing so would require sending Jacob to daycare, something I knew he was not ready for. So earning money from home was the next best option. Although I went to school to be a teacher, art had always been my first love. Staying home with Jacob jumpstarted my art career. God blessed the endeavor, providing me not only with many jobs and projects, but also with the ability to be a stay-at-home mom.

When it was time for Jacob to go to school, many counseled me that he would probably need to be in a special program or homeschooled. But the local school worked with us. Jacob's first grade teacher, knowing that he needed a sense of safety and structure, designed a storybook for him with large pictures of himself in the school with various teachers. Using this, she would tell Jacob to go to the page of the classroom they were currently in, such as his "library page," when they were in the library. This helped him with transitions. She also let me work with him and sit with him in the classroom until the other students arrived.

As his first grade year progressed, sitting with him went to standing by the door, and then waiting down the hall. Finally, on the last day of the school year, I only walked him to the front door of the school. It was thrilling to see him overcoming his fears. He was not only surviving, but also thriving in school. I couldn't wait to share this exciting news with the women in my Moms In Prayer group. They had all been praying along with me that Jacob would make the necessary transition into public school. We all rejoiced in seeing how God was answering prayer for Jacob.

Making friends became the next great challenge. Other kids felt uncomfortable around him, because he often shook his hands uncontrollably or cried over minor things. It was then that I tried to organize play dates with other moms and kids, so Jacob could find a friend. It really was a struggle for him to feel like he could fit in. His physician told us he would learn to overcome autistic struggles, but that his behavioral tendencies would not change. Jacob would always struggle with loud noises, sudden changes, and staying on task.

So Jacob learned to cope with his sensory issues through a sport he loved: running. I couldn't believe my eyes when the boy who cried because of the wind and the lawn mowers positioned himself to run following a piercing gunshot that was sure to be fired. Yes, he was still afraid of the noise, but his determination and faith was his lifeline. And unlike other competitive and team playing sports, this was something he could really finally do! It was exciting to see his confidence increase, and with it, his friends. By his senior year of high school, we found it hard to find family time because he always had something to do with others.

During this final year of high school, we saw him overcome the social and behavioral obstacles of Autism and flourish in school. Jacob worked hard to keep his grades up. He easily took twice as long to finish his assignments and would come home after school and sit in the same chair for hours to complete his homework.

His diligence to attend to his studies, in spite of his disabilities, resulted in a grade point average of almost 3.9. His disability actually helped him make good friends because his love and kindness came from him having a high sensitivity to the people around him.

He began to desire becoming a physical therapist. When we took him to look at colleges, the program he wanted to get into was very competitive, demanding, and required seven years of college education. Yet he was absolutely resolute in his decision.

As the decision for going to college came down to our ability to provide finances, we received a phone call that a dear friend, Myrna, had passed away. Now Myrna and her husband, Dick, who had passed away a year earlier, never acted as if they had much money. But they had apparently saved diligently, wanting to be a blessing to our boys, and had left an inheritance for our two sons.

One month before Jacob's senior graduation, I found myself handing each son a check, reminding them that God was making a way for them to go to college. Their eyes widened as they looked down at $50,000 while being told, "more is coming."

Though not every prayer has been answered in my life, God's gifts are always good and He does hear our prayers. The little boy that would not separate from me, and could not be around many people, now has a big heart for people, for life, and for God. He knows that it was Him alone who saw him through it all.

My entire family, including all those who have prayed with me for Jacob over the years, have learned so much from him about what it means to trust God. We can say wholeheartedly that God has a hope and a future for all who call on Him.

"For I know the plan that I have for you, declares the LORD, plans for welfare and not for calamity to give you a future and a hope."
Jeremiah 29:11 (NASB)

25

Finding Rest

Adam Neal

It was 1962 when the doctor looked at me and said: "My prescription for you is this, get rest and a change of pace."

I was a 30-year-old sales manager for a company with high expectations and quotas to meet. Despite working day and night, I wasn't producing enough. My boss would tell me, "Thanks at least for the try." The anxiety and exhaustion grew and grew until it became more than I could handle.

I knew the doctor was right; rest was desperately needed: *but how could I "rest" with a wife and two small children to support?* Slowing down to take a breather did not seem financially possible. So I worked harder, becoming more exhausted, full of fear, and eventually distrustful of everyone, including Amy, my wife. Finally, I became too weak to work and it was necessary for me to be admitted for a complete nervous breakdown.

For six weeks, I stayed in the hospital to recover. During this time, I asked God for His healing touch. These weeks became God's time to speak to my heart, and give me assurance of His peace and love...allowing my fears to eventually dissipate. I drenched myself in the Scriptures, especially in the Psalms, and committed myself anew to God, getting well, and trusting in people again.

Meanwhile, Amy started working outside of the home to provide for our family's financial needs. The doctor warned her that I might never work again. She was devastated, but nevertheless knew that she was to trust and lean on the Lord for His peace, comfort, and support.

By the end of the six weeks, my health and outlook on life had been restored, so much so, the doctors' released me early and I stopped taking medications. While they may have expected me to relapse, I felt in my heart that God really had healed me.

A week after I was discharged, Amy and I left for California to go to a Christian counseling center. The counseling sessions gave us hope and encouragement that with God's help, we could get back to "normal" and have a fresh start.

Not soon after, I felt well enough to begin applying for jobs. During the application process I was often asked: "Have you ever been hospitalized for mental issues?" My answer would have to be "yes." I had to rise above the stigma of suffering a nervous breakdown. It was not easy, but with God's help, within five years, I became successful in my line of work and throughout the years have received awards for high sales achievements.

But the greatest miracle of all is that God "delivered me from all my fears," as the psalmist David said. This truly was a miracle of healing. I am forever grateful to the Lord for His healing touch.

"I sought the Lord and He heard me and delivered me from all my fears."
Psalm 34:4

———

26

A Prayer, Lord, That I May Pray

Tami Laursen

My daughter, Rachel, was in elementary school when a fellow mother of a student, Barbara, started relentlessly inviting me to a weekly prayer meeting called Moms In Prayer to pray for our children and their school's faculty.

Now I loved prayer. I knew this would be about building a relationship with my Heavenly Father while also building relationships with people by learning to trust God together. Of course I wanted to pray with these women—for our children and their teachers. Yet each time she invited me, I found myself declining, making lame excuses in my head as to why I couldn't go, such as, "I want my Friday's free." I came to discover, however, that my real fear was the intimidating thought that if I went to Moms In Prayer, I would have to pray out loud with other people listening.

I declined the invitation for 18 months, but Barbara was persistent. I finally caved in and told her I would show up at the next meeting.

As I drove there, I wrestled with my insecurities about speaking and praying to God out loud. But when I walked into the room, I was met by some of the most welcoming and encouraging women. Barbara turned out to be the coordinator for that Moms In Prayer group. As we started praying together, I clearly saw these women were real prayer warriors. Over time, through receiving God's grace and sharing part of my prayer life with these women, I was able to face my fears of praying out loud.

When Rachel was in eighth grade, my husband's job required us to move from Puyallup, Washington to Clackamas, Oregon. Missing my Moms In Prayer group in Puyallup tremendously, I began asking God to help me find another group of prayer partners. One day, nearly a year later, I was leaving Rachel's high school when I heard someone call my name. I turned around to a woman who introduced herself and said: "I want to invite you to our Moms In Prayer group."

My jaw dropped. I was so excited that I rushed home to tell Rachel the news. Yet again, and unsuspectingly, I began creating excuses as to why I could not make it to the meetings. They were the same as before: mere insecurities around the idea of praying out loud in a room full of women whom I did not know.

For three months, I didn't go.

Yet during this time, God removed my pride and excuses. I realized this fear about praying out loud shouldn't hold me back. He put a true longing in my heart to be in authentic relationship with fellow women so we could pray for our children. I had to go to Moms In Prayer in faith that God would provide those kinds of friendships while teaching me how to pray.

Like déjà vu, I walked through the front door of the Clackamas Moms In Prayer group and was greeted by a loving and enthusiastic woman named Suzanne, with whom I instantly connected. All the other women were genuine and loving, and I could hardly wait to go back the next week. As I got in my car to leave that first meeting, my heart felt full of gratitude to God for taking me there.

During our meetings, we were encouraged to pray with someone different each week, in which I was always amazed with how God seemed to place me with just the right woman to pray with and get to know better. All 20 of us have come to know each other better through praying God's Word for our children and seeing God faithfully interceding in our lives.

All too soon, Rachel headed to college at the same time as many of the other mom's children in our group. Each week, as Rachel shared prayer requests with me, this group of women became vital in my life. Their passion for prayer helped me leave the burdens I brought through the door with the Lord.

Week after week, we saw Him provide scholarships to colleges, acceptances to medical schools, heal family relationships, and so much more.

Though most of our children are now adults, we still meet on a weekly basis during the school year to pray for them. Suzanne and I have been prayer warriors and dear friends ever since that very first meeting. We have laughed and cried together, and prayed our children through their high school and college years.

I stand in awe of God and His ability to help me have a personal relationship with Him and others through the power of prayer. I realize how God, the only perfect parent, provides His children's best when I, as an imperfect earthy parent, learn to depend on Him. He has taught and assured me of who I really am to and in Him. He is a trustworthy God in whom I can leave my fear and insecurity in His loving and capable Hands—even about how to pray.

"Two are better than one, because they have a good return for their work: If one falls down, his friend can help him up."
Ecclesiastes 4:9-10

—

27

Light House Down the Street

Vernon L. Thompson

"**P**reacher, we need help. Food, clothes, housing, money—anything would help us."

These were the words of two men, dressed in rumpled overalls and denim shirts, standing in my office at Calvary United Methodist Church in Annapolis, Maryland. It was a hot summer day in 1988.

I soon came to find out that they were eastern shore fishermen who were newly out of work and had been sleeping under a nearby street bridge just outside our church doors. After listening to their stories and giving them some groceries and vouchers for lodging, I determined to take their plight before the Annapolis Ministerial Association, of which I was the current president.

The need was obvious. Although each of the six downtown churches in the association had its own assistance program, we needed to unite our efforts if we were going to effectively tackle homelessness and hunger in downtown Annapolis. A task force soon began developing a plan, and a makeshift respite, which consisted of only six cots, was immediately set up in St. Anne's Episcopal Church's Parish House in the center of the city.

The other five churches took turns housing the homeless on their premises, especially during the winter. Three years later, through donations, gifts, and grants, the association purchased an abandoned storefront building with apartments overhead on West Street in downtown Annapolis. It was the ideal location because it was in the midst of the business section, which could provide employment; it was on the main city bus line, which provided easy and affordable transportation; and lastly, it held the prospect of expansion. Thus was born Light House, a homeless prevention support center, which served 15 residential clients and provided lunches to the community.

However, the center was only two city blocks from a prestigious enclave of stately older homes filled with wealthy owners. Many of these homeowners were also the movers and shakers of Annapolitan life. They claimed that it adversely affected property values, that an unwanted clientele were roaming their streets, and that "there were no housing or hunger problems in the capitol city of Maryland."

So they sued to cancel the project.

Weeks before the case came to trial, we sent prayer appeals, not only to the Annapolis churches, but also around the vicinity. Prayer vigils were set. In the end, the Annapolis Area Ministries won the case.

Soon after, we planned a mile long dedication parade down Main Street on a Sunday morning, which would begin at St. Anne's Parish House and end at the Light House. This was to also publicize the fact that the center was opening and functioning. However, we were denied the parade permit because the city said it had no funds for the police to monitor the event. Again, we set out a prayer appeal, wanting the community to realize that the center would be a wonderful, and necessary, addition to Annapolis.

On Saturday, the day before the dedication, we received a notice from the city saying that adequate funds had been given to cover the cost of police monitoring the parade. Later, we discovered that the same lawyer who filed the first lawsuit to stop the project had contributed the funds!

At the beginning of this project, I felt that each minister was clothed in the sandals of David, the shepherd boy, going up against the giant: Goliath, i.e., the Establishment. There was a vast difference between our dream and our plan. As they say, an effective plan is "S.M.A.R.T.," by which I mean specific, measurable, achievable, relevant to your problem, and contains a time line. Our dreams were vague achings of the heart, which we turned into a plan by faith and prayer—"for the battle is the Lords," as David said.

After successfully completing an $8.4 million fundraising campaign in 2010, the Lord graciously blessed the Light House with a new 24,000 square foot facility with the capacity to house 30 men, 15 women, and five families with up to 20 children, and a large commercial kitchen. The pantry program began distributing 250 bag-lunches each day and 400 bags of groceries each month. In 2011, the Building Employment Success Training (B.E.S.T) program was established to provide job-training skills, which could help residents find sustainable employment and ultimately permanent housing.

This truly was the Lord's doing. It was Him who made a way for us to go from a six-cot beginning in a parish house lobby to the multi-million dollar facility supported by the whole community today.

"For the battle is the Lord's, and He will give you into our hands."
1 Samuel 17:47 (NASB)

———

Vernon L. Thompson is the former pastor of Calvary United Methodist Church, Annapolis, Maryland. He is also a member of founding board of directors of Light House Shelter.

28

New Memories
Carol Moyer

O ur son Jay has always had a lot of friends with his fun, loving "salesman" personality; and fortunately my husband, Jim, and I were always able to be his friend, too. As he grew up, he seemed to grow more open with us, regularly having heart-to-heart conversations. Jay even won a business trip to San Diego and amazingly chose me, his mother, to come with him. Later he took his dad when he won a trip to Bermuda. That's the way we were.

One day, not long after Jay was married, he came to me and asked about the way we disciplined him. When he and his sister were younger, Jim and I tried our best to love and train them well. We certainly didn't do everything perfectly, and we've humbly admitted to many errors, yet we tried to love our children and apply parental discipline with discernment and love. So as soon as Jay brought this up, I was confused; he had never seemed so affected by these memories. He then told me that his wife had prompted him to see a counselor about his past. She told him he had abandonment issues, and that he was "unable to cope with life." She was somewhat threatening their marriage if he didn't go to the counselor. When she picked out a counselor, he felt compelled to go.

That day, Jay asked me to come with him to his counseling session. So the hesitation—the incredible angst—I was feeling about this had nothing to do with the counseling itself, but with the topic that had been brought up out of the clear blue.

The office was black and dark. Within a minute, the counselor told me exactly where to sit and that I could not speak a word, ask a question, or seek to understand. I was just to listen. She then began telling me of Jay's internal struggles with the way we disciplined him as a child, and how those things had caused him great damage in his ability to cope with life.

"You have ruined him," she said to me, with further statements of how I was a "bad influence" and that all the encouraging notes I wrote to Jay were unhealthy because "they caused Jay to feel uncomfortable and uneasy."

Yet Jay had told me many times "thank you" for the notes of encouragement and praise. He had written me letters telling me that I was his example. He had involved me in his life since his young adulthood.

This counselor was describing Jay as a person I did not know. There was no truth in her words—it was all a blatant attack on me.

I was not a perfect parent by any means. Yet throughout my adult relationship with Jay, I sought to understand him. I cared about where he was coming from when we discussed these past hurts. I'd birthed, raised, and loved him for 30 years! But this was simply confusing! I felt angry, attacked, and betrayed.

The counselor then told us that neither Jim nor I were to have any contact with him or his family. No communication. No letters. No notes of affirmation. No seeing our one-year-old granddaughter. I walked out of the office certain this was the darkest experience I had ever had.

Driving home, I cried my heart out, devastated, angry, and confused. It felt as if my heart had a sword through it, twisted until I could no longer stand the pain. Yet in hindsight, I am glad the Lord guided me to go to the counselor with Jay because it confirmed what I saw and felt earlier—that this situation was a demonic attack.

Jim and I immediately went straight to a Christian counselor and friend, Alan. After hearing our story, he wisely said: "This *is* a spiritual battle. Go home, get a prayer team, and start praying." We called and emailed a number of friends, who graciously agreed to partner with us in prayer for the power of Satan to be broken and for our relationship with Jay to be restored. Meanwhile, we tried to reconcile with Jay and see if we could talk things through. Two times we reached out, only to be unpleasantly reminded we were to have no communication with him.

For six months, I cried daily. The pain and loss were deep. I began spending every day in long periods of reading the Word to get my feet on level ground. As His presence became my sustenance, and His Word my perspective, Jesus reminded me of a time earlier in life when a counselor said: "The person who has hurt you will come out of it. When they do, have a ready heart to receive them. Otherwise, you'll want say, 'you owe me because you hurt me.' Let the Holy Spirit keep your heart clean." So I started working on daily forgiving Jay, his wife, and the counselor.

But it still didn't explain the darkness of the situation. After about a year, and through a divine appointment, the Lord led me to a friend who instantly identified the type of psychological counseling Jay had received and which ensnared him: False Memory Syndrome. False Memory Syndrome is a condition in which a person's identity and relationships are affected by memories that are factually wrong, but strongly believed. In our case, the counselor led Jay to believe our disciplines damaged him for life, and that the only way for him to survive and overcome those memories was for us to be removed. My prayers for Jay now had a target: I prayed for God to heal and restore his *right* and *true* memories back to him.

Two and half years after the awful meeting with Jay's counselor, Jim and I took our annual day trip north to hike and see the beautiful, fall-colored trees. At the time, Jay was living in the area, so I asked Jim: "I know we are forbidden to go by Jay's house or to see anyone in their family, but I have to go by and just see Jay's house and where they live."

"I had the same thought," said Jim. So we turned off the main road, in fear and trepidation, and began proceeding slowly down their street. Lo and behold, on the opposite side of the street, a nanny was pushing a stroller with our two granddaughters inside.

"Jim," I said, "turn around and drive slowly past them. I need to see my granddaughters. I promise to duck down and be quiet." We turned around and started back slowly. But just after we drove past the nanny and the two girls, Jay came around the corner on his bike!

"We're busted!" said Jim.

Both of us knew we were not to be there and could only wonder what Jay might say or do to us. Jay rode right up to the driver's side of the car. Scared out of our minds, Jim rolled the window down just a crack, only enough to talk to Jay. To our amazement, Jay started talking about his new bike, the suspension, and his bike ride!

"Don't you want to come back to the house and come in?" he said. We were stunned. Without another word, Jim quickly turned the car around.

"Lord—help!! We need You more than ever now," we both cried aloud in prayer. We cautiously pulled onto the driveway, got out of the car, and walked into the garage with Jay. His wife and our two grand-daughters, Skye and Caylee, were standing there. Before we knew it, Jay turned to his three-year-old, Skye, and said: "Wouldn't you like Momo (my grandmother name) to read you a story?"

I followed Skye to her bedroom, sat down on her bed—still in shock and fighting back tears—and read her a story. While I was reading the story, Jay appeared and said: "Don't you want Momo to read you another story?"

Several stories later, I was trying to leave because I was uncomfortable, nervous, and unsure of what might happen next. Jim had gone to the car for the same reasons. We were aware that Jay had told us twice that we were to never be at their house. *Did the rules of this game just change?* I wondered.

But Jay stopped me as I was trying to leave, saying he wanted to show me something they had done on their new home. While I was going with him, he looked at me with "his smile"—all of you mothers know what I mean. I knew it would be okay when I saw "the Jay smile."

When we finally left, Jim and I were in shock and cried and rejoiced as we drove out to see the leaves, and for most of the way home.

We knew that only through our prayers, and the prayers of our faithful friends, could Jay be set free from Satan and the hands of this counselor.

Jay invited us back into his life as if it had never happened. And the Lord answered my prayers. I didn't feel a need to say, "You were wrong" or hold him hostage to my pain. I could have rejected his acceptance, but instead my heart was able to receive it. It was only by the grace of God that I was able to move on with a clean heart.

Jim and I could have never imagined the way the Lord began reconciling us with our son. Jay has encouraged us to visit him and his family anytime we can. During our visits, Jim, Jay, and I have had heart-to-hearts just as before. We have our son back and can only credit the Lord for a complete restoration.

It is the Lord who brings healing and restoration. His power is at work in each of us and sovereignly in our most painful situations, proving His ways wonderful, complete, and beyond anything we could ever ask or imagine. He truly cares for us and graciously hears and answers our prayers.

"So there is hope for your descendants, declares the Lord.
Your children will return to their own land."
Jeremiah 31:16-17

———

29

An Unscathed Mind
Keri Jackson

It was a beautiful, mid-September Saturday morning. My husband, Tom, had just left to take our son, Brady, to his Junior High football pre-game warm ups where I'd meet them an hour later for the game.

As soon as they left, it was one of those coveted Mom moments of sudden peace and quiet in the house. I was all alone in the house as our eldest, Emily, was involved in her first year of college, while our other two teenage daughters, Whitney and Bethany, were at an overnight cross-country meet together. I relaxed into the morning, took a shower, and put on my make-up with time to spare. It felt like a day at the spa until my cell phone rang. It was my neighbor, Desiree.

"Well, hi there, Desiree," I said in a cheery voice. "Happy Saturday—"

"No, Keri! Listen to me!" she interrupted. "It's Tom...he's been in an accident!"

Fear gripped me as she continued: "I was on the road to the high school when I encountered his car coming toward me and stopping only inches from mine. My son Levi cried out, 'Mom! That's Tom's car... and that is Tom slumped over the wheel.'"

She continued: "The paramedics are rushing him to the closest ER. You need to leave right now and meet them there...now!"

God...no...no...NO! Shaking in disbelief and shock, I collected my thoughts so I could function enough to get in the car. Heading down the hill from my neighborhood, I prayed over and over again: *God, please don't take Tom...please don't take Tom...please don't take Tom!*

Paramedics met me at the entrance of the ER and directed me to a room on the left. There I saw Tom lying on the emergency table, surrounded by doctors and nurses working tirelessly to revive him.

Tom had suffered from a cardiac arrest, I learned. They needed to stabilize his brain immediately through a medicated coma and apply a full body 24-hour ice blanket over his unconscious body. The coma coupled with the applied ice would be crucial if he had any chance of escaping brain damage—that is, should he survive.

After calling key parents to notify our kids in their respective places as to what had happened, I walked down to the waiting room of ICU and landed on a chair in an emotional heap. From there, I called my dearest friend Beth, who in turn notified our friends, church, and extended family to ask them to start praying for Tom.

Never before had I leaned on Jesus like I did that day. The fears of becoming a single mom managing a household alone and raising a son and daughters to full adulthood were daunting.

As word began to spread, the ICU waiting room became a house of prayer and support. By nightfall there were up to 40 people there to love, support, and pray for Tom and our family. As one person would leave, another would come. Our church was truly being the Church to us; Pastor Maddox never left our side. Emily's closest friends came to the hospital for her support. Whitney and Bethany were prayed over on their athletic bus, and then transferred to the hospital from the coast by Moms In Prayer families. Brady was offered diversion from fears of losing his Dad by spending the night at a close friend's home.

Additional families mobilized meals to be sent to the hospital in the following days and our pantry at home soon became filled to overflowing.

Our physical, mental, and spiritual needs were being met. We lacked nothing, and peace ensued.

Later that evening, I was finally allowed to see Tom. I walked into the room where he lay in a coma, completely unprepared to see him hooked up to all the equipment with tubes down his throat.

With a Bible in hand from the waiting room, I turned to Psalm 139, knowing if God created Tom in secret, He was also fully aware what was happening within his body right now. *This will be Your story, God,* I prayed. I began taking comfort in the precious thoughts that God had toward Tom, believing Tom's days were ordained and written in God's book before one of them came to pass.

Back in the waiting room, when a woman sitting beside me learned of my husband's story, she said: "I can't believe how calm and peaceful you are." I told her I couldn't explain it either; I just knew God was going to care for us and I trusted Him.

After 48 hours, it was time for Tom to come out of the medicated coma. Despite ICU guidelines that only two people can be in his room at a time, I asked his attending nurse, whom we found out was a Romanian Christian, for permission for all the friends and family currently in the waiting room to come beside Tom's bed. She not only agreed to this, but also asked if she could have the honor of leading out in prayer for him. As we surrounded his bedside, I could sense each heart surrendered for God's will to be done. I clung to the prayers spoken in faith: "In Jesus' name, we ask that Tom be protected from any ill effect as he awakes. Amen."

As Tom began waking up and stabilizing, he showed signs of confusion as to why and how he had landed in the hospital. We continued to have conversations with him, and the Tom we knew and loved prior to the incident came back. The paramedics conveyed that they rarely see this: of the five percent that survive a cardiac arrest, most are left with varying degrees of extreme brain damage.

Even though Tom would need two stints and an implanted medical device, this was a small price to pay for mental wholeness coming through what cardiologists call a "widow maker" event.

Through Tom's most tentative hours, and in nights of my personal unrest, the Lord spoke and reminded me that He is the great I Am and that He had Tom in the palm of His hand.

I have since found out many ways in which God orchestrated Tom's deliverance that day. Desiree was providentially on the scene of the accident and onlookers with CPR certification and equipment stopped.

Paramedics had delayed their travel for another cup of coffee, which put them only two minutes from the incident. The closest ER hospital was the one that pioneered the ice blanket treatment for brain stabilization post trauma. Finally, Tom's second transfer to another hospital put him into the hands of one of the most respected electro-cardiologists. In everything, God's timing was perfect timing.

The verse the Lord gave Tom while in the hospital, and which has become our life charge is Psalm 50:15b: "And you will call upon Me in your day of trouble, I will deliver you and you will honor Me."

Lord, may we never forget and always be reminded that in life or in death You never leave us alone. You always provide. You are always faithful!

"And you will call upon Me in your day of trouble,
I will deliver you and you will honor Me."
Psalm 50:15b

———

30

Thin Glass Prayers
Marty Trammell

"Who do we know that has any money?" My young wife, Linda, dropped her head and slid into the green vinyl dinette chair, tearing a clump of yellowed foam from a rip its side.

"No one, I guess."

"Then what are we going to do? Move back into an apartment?"

I glanced away from her tears, dragging my eyes around the duplex we were renting from a friend. It had started to feel like home.

"Are you sure we can't squeeze more from our budget?" Her warm, brown eyes repeated the look I'd seen many times in the past month.

"Well, we could take the food stamps; we do qualify. Maybe we should change our minds and sign up. It would save us the amount we need to pay for the rent increase."

She looked around the duplex as if for the last time. "No. They're meant for the poor—and we're not starving. There's got to be another way."

I closed the sliding glass door behind me and watched her as she lowered her head. The thin glass separated our prayers.

Faded caramel deck-paint peeled beneath my shoes as I stepped toward the large Styrofoam computer-packaging container that Linda had pulled from the neighborhood recycling bin. She'd turned it into a sandbox for our two-year-old son, Justin, and his baby brother, Christopher. I sat with Justin on the worn edge of the box.

"Daddy, watch this!" Justin lifted a small plastic block, revealing a perfect square of sand.

"Daddy, this is the house where Mary and Jophus put baby Jesus." The whites of his eyes glistened in the deepening dusk.

Justin loved the deck and the sandbox. He'd play for hours in his make believe world of sand castles and Hot Wheels. As I watched him play, the thought of moving back into a smaller apartment hopelessly fell like grains of sand between my fingers.

The following weeks faded into the gray clouds of fall, as the raise in rent approached. The salary scale at the small Christian college where I taught had frozen with the dwindling enrollment. No answer there. The youth pastor position at the small country church we'd decided to serve at could only provide enough to cover the gas expenses. No answer there. The secretarial position my wife had left to stay at home with our sons provided no option for work at home. No answer there. Narnia's "always winter, but never Christmas" punctuated my prayers.

One day my wife asked me, "Guess who called this morning after you left for work? Doreen."

"Your friend from high school? How's she doing?" I noticed a small tear as Linda turned toward the kitchen.

"She's fine."

I laid a stack of college writing papers on the country blue recliner Linda had reupholstered the year before and put my arms around her. Her shoulders shook as she spoke.

"She said we shouldn't be renting, that it's smarter to buy a house. She and Kenny just bought one in Seattle."

"Honey, she doesn't know our situation. I'm sure she wouldn't have said anything if she'd known we were struggling."

I stared over her shoulder at the butcher-block counter top. "We can't get a loan, we can't buy a house, we can't afford the rent, we can't..."

I slumped into a dinette chair hoping she didn't see in my eyes the fears that plagued my thoughts. There was nothing else to do but finally force myself to make the decision to move into an apartment or leave the ministry.

Linda picked up a sippy cup Justin had left in the kitchen. "What do you want for dinner?" Her words trailed off into an almost silent evening.

The next morning, the pulsating phone shattered the Saturday morning stillness. I rolled over and lifted the receiver.

"Hi, is this Marty? This is Marilyn Dorn, Doreen's mom. Can we talk for a moment?" I sat up and stuffed a pillow behind my head.

"Sure."

"I was wondering if you could do me a favor? I invest in real estate here in Seattle and I've done quite well, so I was thinking about expanding down the I-5 corridor into Salem."

"Okay."

"Well, I was wondering if you could find two or three starter homes for me. I could use the additional investments. I'd remodel them and sell them for a profit."

"Okay. I'm sure I could talk to an agent and mail you some pictures and descriptions. Is that what you're looking for?"

"That would be perfect. Are you sure it wouldn't be too much to ask?" I slid lower into the bed.

"No, we'd be glad to help."

"Okay. Thanks. I'll call you back in a couple of weeks." As I set the phone in its cradle, I couldn't help but wonder why Doreen's mom, Marilyn, would call two days after Doreen. I'd never met either of them and Linda hadn't seen Marilyn in several years.

"Who was it?" Linda's barely open eyes focused slowly.

"Doreen's mom wants us to send her pictures of a few houses in Salem. She invests in real estate now."

"Real estate? Why did she call us?"

"Something about the I-5 corridor and rising house prices. Did Doreen say anything about this?"

"No, but that's kind of weird, isn't it?"

I sat straight up and threw the covers back. "Linda, what if she wants us to help with the remodels and what if she lets us rent from her or live in the homes until they sell or what if..." Linda sat up, too.

The next week, I mailed three sets of pictures and descriptions for the fixer-uppers. And we prayed. Not just our three-meals-a-day prayers, but during nearly every break in our routines.

Three days later Marilyn called. As she rehearsed the normal greetings, my mind raced. Just the sound of her voice filled my head with hope.

Please, let us fix these up for her, I prayed as she finished her hello. I glanced across the Berber carpet at Linda, who was reading to Chris and Justin. Her head was bowed.

"Well, I would like to discuss something with you, if now's a good time."

"Now's a great time, Mrs. Dorn, we're just playing with the boys."

"Oh, okay. Well, the reason I wanted to talk with you, Marty, is that—I don't want to offend you in any way... I know you're both serving the Lord and well, like I said earlier—I've made some money in Seattle flipping houses. And well, lately, I've been helping young couples in the ministry get into their first homes. So, when Doreen told me you were still renting, I checked up on your salary at the college. I hope that's okay."

"Sure, anyone can get a copy of the pay scale. I'm not sure I understand why though." I stretched the phone cord over the table and sat at the dinette.

Please, Lord, if we could only help her remodel these homes and have a place for Justin and Chris to play.

"Well, looking at your salary and the loan amount you'd be able to qualify for, I'm figuring you'll need at least $14,000 to get into one of the homes you sent descriptions of."

"14,000? We already tried to qualify for various home loans, Mrs. Dorn, we can't, we just—"

"Oh, I know, Doreen told me the same day I was praying about finding another young couple to help out. It's not a loan, Marty, I want to give you the money."

"Give us the money?" Thick thoughts of renting and remodeling blocked her words.

"Well, if that's alright with you, that is."

"Um, with me? $14,000?" Linda sat Chris on the carpet and stood.

"Mrs. Dorn, I don't know what to say. This is more than we could even hope for." Linda stepped beside me, her eyes pulled at my words.

"I don't know what to say. Thank you. What's the next step?" I stood and put my arm around Linda's waist and whispered, "She wants to help us buy one of the homes."

Linda and I sat at the same table that night, poring over the same budget. The worn pages where we'd written figures and erased them over and over were the same. Only this time we penciled in $14,000 on a line that before had been empty. The line item read, "Our Home."

The day we signed papers, we mailed a thank-you to Mrs. Dorn. As we opened the door to the mailbox, a letter sat waiting. Linda reached for it.

"It's from Marilyn," she said, tearing the end off the envelope.

"Dear Marty and Linda, I can't tell you how happy it made me to be able to help a young couple continue in the ministry. I've enclosed a check as a house warming gift. . ."

"A house-warming gift? She just helped us buy the house. Why would she send a house warming gift?"

"I don't know," Linda smiled warmly, "but do you think we can do anything with $1,000?"

> "I waited patiently for the Lord to help me, and He turned to me and heard my cry. He lifted me out of the pit of despair, out of the mud and the mire. He set my feet on solid ground and steadied me as I walked along."
> Psalm 40:1-3 (NLT)

Originally published in *Guideposts*. Edited and published with permission.

Marty Trammell enjoys the outdoors, reading, and serving with his "amazing" wife, Linda, and family and friends at Corban University, Valley Baptist Church, and redeemingrelationships.com.

31

Twenty Years of Wondering
Wanda MacLean

It was 8:00 p.m. in Budapest, Hungary in the fall of 1994. I had just settled into my seat inside the sliding doors of the subway. It felt good to have reprieve from the cold autumn air, and I had five minutes to indulge my people-watching habit before my final stop. There was a pretty blonde woman with a sweet little girl sitting across from me. I thought, *Are you really a blonde, or do you dye your hair?*

To my surprise, her voice interrupted my silent inquiry.

"Excuse me, do you speak English?" She sounded American. Then to a greater surprise, she asked, "Is your name Wanda?" I desperately scrambled to recognize this stranger.

"It's me, Cindy Larson," she said.

My mind raced back to 1974 where I first met Cindy in high school. After that, we entered the same nursing program and went to our OB (obstetrics) rotation together. Abortions had just become legal, but our nursing school avoided talking about it. We were not even allowed onto the hospital floor where abortion patients were staying.

One day, however, our nursing instructor led just the two of us, me and Cindy, into an exclusive room.

"I could lose my job for showing you this," she said.

Cindy and I found ourselves standing above a sterile stainless steel counter. Lying in the middle was a little baby with her hand touching her cheek. Her mother had just had a saline abortion at five months gestation, and this was her lifeless little girl.

"I could never have an abortion," Cindy exclaimed. It was a powerful and sad moment for the both of us.

Cindy and I soon became friends. She told me she had a church upbringing, but stopped attending since college, so I began praying for her walk with the Lord. One day, the Lord gave me an opportunity at one of our lunch breaks to share my testimony with her.

"I admire you for your faith," she said, "but I'm not ready to do that. I'm having a lot of fun right now."

I continued to pray for her. One year later, we sat in a park and I shared the Gospel with her again. Her response was warm, but no different than the last.

"Thanks, but I'm not ready for this," she said.

Now 20 years later, in a city of 2.2 million people, we found ourselves ascending a steep elevator from the subway to bustling Budapest's Moscow Square.

I told her that I was a missionary and my purpose in Hungary was to tell people about the hope of Jesus.

"What are you doing in Budapest, Cindy?" I asked on the elevator steps.

"My husband and I just arrived as new missionaries," she said. "Wanda, I accepted Christ about one month after we last met. I've always wanted to find you and thank you for sharing the Gospel with me."

One week later, Cindy and I met at my favorite coffee shop and she told me more of her story. She told me the sad news that she had had two abortions after our time in nursing school. One can only imagine the torment she experienced after that, and yet this is what drew her into the forgiving arms of Jesus, where she experienced His redeeming peace.

God let me see the answer to prayer for Cindy's salvation 20 years after the fact, and 9,000 miles away from where it all began. But truly, it did not even start with my encounter with Cindy in nursing school, but years before when she was skillfully wrought in her mother's womb.

"For You formed my inward parts; You knitted me together in my mother's womb. I praise You, for I am fearfully and wonderfully made. Wonderful are Your works; my soul knows it very well."
Psalm 139:13-14

———

32

Heavens Invading Surabaya

Josue Ramirez

One day, when my friends Julie, Moush, and I were on a mission trip in Surabaya, Indonesia, we had a few hours to spare. Desiring that God would move powerfully through us with His compassion and love, we went to Surabaya's main village store and bought a lot of food and candy, and then asked God for a clue as to where to go.

Now the Holy Spirit speaks in both creative and mysterious ways. As we were praying for direction about who He wanted us to love, we felt God bring to our minds the word "chicken."

What did that mean? we asked ourselves. We continued walking through streets of Surabaya and asking God to show us where He wanted us to go. Suddenly, we saw a chicken walking down the sidewalk.

With our bags of candy and food in hand, the three of us started following the chicken as it walked along. The chicken turned into a dark alley, so we followed it down there. When we came onto the other side of the alley, we found ourselves in the courtyard of a small Muslim "kampung" neighborhood, which is similar to a slum.

As we entered the kampung, 20 children and their parents came out to the courtyard to meet us. We started giving them the food and candy we'd bought. No one in the kampung spoke English, and yet we found a way to communicate to ask if anyone had any sickness or injuries so we could pray for them to be healed.

An old lady came forward. Sitting in a chair in front of us, she looked at us and pointed to her knees, and then to a spot on her back. Believing

God wanted to move in compassion and love toward this woman, we began praying for her.

After a short, minute-long prayer, the woman stood up and started jumping around. Jesus had completely healed her knees and back! She hugged and kissed me on the cheek, and for the next hour she was jumping up and down with much joy.

Right after that healing, five more ladies with similar knee and back injuries lined up for prayer. As my team and I prayed, we saw God touch and heal each of their back and knee injuries.

The neighborhood life erupted, and the ladies started taking us to others in the kampung who needed prayer for healing. A few men had shoulder and arm injuries from hard work and labor. Jesus touched and healed every man's injury.

Heaven invaded this neighborhood; it was as if the pages from the book of Acts had come alive in this little kampung. For two hours, we celebrated and jumped around with the village children. At the time, it was hard to explain to them the "Who" that had healed them. But the next day, we came back to the kampung with a translator.

Through our translator, the first lady we prayed for with severe knee and back pain told us she had been in pain for many years, which had always robbed her of a good night's sleep. She went to doctors and took medicine, but nothing worked. Then she told us she had slept well the night before with no pain whatsoever! For first time in years, all her pain was gone.

Through our translator, we asked her, "Who do you think healed you?"

She pointed at us and said the people believed we had "powers from the sky."

We explained it wasn't us—it wasn't Josue, Julie, or Moush. It was Jesus, the Living Son of God in Heaven. The people knew the name of Jesus from the Koran. When the lady heard this, she started to tear up.

She wanted prayer again, in fear the pain might come back. But we told her through our translator that our Jesus in heaven had completely healed her and that He was showing her how much He loves her. With endless tears coming down her face, she told us "thank you for coming to pray."

Throughout the rest of our trip, we continued to follow up with this neighborhood. Because of security reasons, we sensitively and carefully shared the Good News individually with each person who had been touched by the love of the Father through healing that day. It was through our Father's love and compassion that He healed them, and we give Him all the glory.

"And [Jesus] sent them out to proclaim the kingdom of God
and to heal the sick."
Luke 9:2

———

Josué Ramirez is a man passionate about pandas, Jesus, evangelism, healing and revival. He trains young adults in missions and discipleship.

33

Surprising Packages
Betsy S.

Answers to prayer don't always arrive in the packaging I expect. I grew up living one of those ridiculously blessed lives—the sort that caused people to doubt my honesty and push for a sign of unacknowledged disaster.

Living in northern California where the sun shone almost daily, I had a loving and stable Christian family, incredible health (I rarely even got a cold), and a wonderfully supportive community of friends. My husband came from a more challenging background and often said I "grew up in a bubble." But after our two children were born, an "acknowledged disaster" appeared out of nowhere: I started to experience minor seizures.

Doctors were baffled; tests and scans of all kinds didn't reveal any problematic issues and almost all anti-seizure drugs were rendered useless. A medical explanation was never found. Discouragement crept into my life as I realized my unusually good health was not likely to return anytime soon. But thankfully, after more than 13 years of multiple medications and extensive treatment, my seizure disorder dramatically improved and my hope and belief for complete healing was restored.

However, I currently still experience minor, infrequent, and one-minute "absence seizures." Just prior to a seizure, I experience an aura, a neurological warning that allows me approximately 20 seconds to prepare myself before the seizure comes on.

Despite the odds of safety working strongly in my favor, I chose to restrict my driving and carefully monitor my activities. I certainly wasn't tempted to take up scuba diving, but I occasionally drove short distances from my house for work and errands.

"Aren't you afraid of having a seizure when you drive?" a friend once asked me.

"No," I replied. "When I get in the car, I simply ask God to protect myself and other drivers. Just as Jesus cried out on the cross, I also pray, 'Father, into Your hands I commit my spirit.'"

One day I had to drive for a work errand. On the way home, I had an aura as I was exiting the freeway. I immediately saw there was no place to pull over on the exit ramp before the seizure occurred. As I approached the three-way stoplight on a busy main street, the seizure began.

My speed increased and I hit the car in front of me, smashing the driver's bumper up to his back seat. Next, I crossed all four lanes of traffic on that road, jumping the raised median. I hit another car on the opposite side of the street and spun it onto the sidewalk. Finally, I went over an embankment and hit a tree straight on. When I regained consciousness less than a minute later, I didn't understand why three distraught people were running up the hill toward me. Because they were running the opposite direction from a restaurant that had been closed for years, my first thought was: "Oh, that's crazy! They should have called ahead to find out if the restaurant was still open." I hadn't yet noticed the tree directly in front of me.

A sweet woman came to my car door window and frantically asked if I was okay. Just as I was telling her I was fine, I noticed the tree a few feet from my face, indicating my situation was less than ideal. I was not pleased to see the hood of my car was wrapped around the tree's trunk. This Good Samaritan told me about the accident and helped me call my husband. Within minutes, police and firefighters arrived and assessed the damage.

My only physical injury was a slightly bruised chin caused by hitting the steering wheel. However, two other drivers and one passenger were involved, and we were all rushed by ambulance to hospital emergency rooms. After an extremely thorough and embarrassing medical exam, my lack of injury was irrefutable. And throughout that intensive ER stay, I prayed for the health and comfort of the other three people involved in the accident.

The next day a policeman who had been at the scene called me to check up on my condition. Both he and the primary doctor who had examined me believed that I should have been seriously injured, if not dead. They simply could not make sense of just a slightly bruised chin. The policeman also reported on the amazingly healthy status of all of us—everyone had been examined and released from the hospital!

"God miraculously protected us," I told the policeman, wanting him to hear that God, because of His love that surpasses understanding, performed this miracle that preserved our lives. "Luck" or "an alignment of the stars" couldn't take credit for this!

I had, of course, assumed that God would protect me *from* a seizure-related car accident. Instead, God protected me *during* a seizure-related car accident.

Now life isn't "the bubble" I enjoyed in the past—and that's difficult. I lost my driver's license, with no current hope of it being returned. Would I choose this frustrating lifestyle? Definitely not! However, I am willing to accept that my brilliantly wise God has a carefully crafted purpose for me. Though I'm not overly excited about it, my new status of restricted freedom is one in which I trust His plan will best be fulfilled.

His intervention that day provides exciting proof of His closeness, compassion, and power. I confidently believe that God stepped in to work miraculously on my behalf. I determine to share my story of God's protection with anyone who will listen: the bank teller, grocery clerk, Costco employee, mail carrier. And now I pray my story of His miraculous rescue causes you to depend upon God's answer to your call, even if His response doesn't seem to fit your desired outcome or packaging.

*"For my thoughts are not your thoughts, neither are
your ways my ways," declares the Lord."*
Isaiah 55:8

———

34

Always Hope
Kathy Collard Miller

M y thoughts were as piercing as the screeching wheels of the train, rumbling past the east coast countryside. *Why did Greg kill himself?* He was a distant relative whom I rarely saw, yet the news of his suicide made tears fill my eyes. *Oh, to be that full of despair.*

But in the past, I had struggled with suicidal feelings. I glanced over at my 28-year-old sleeping daughter, Darcy. If I had acted on those feelings, I wouldn't have the fabulous mother-daughter relationship I now enjoyed with her.

It was 26 years earlier when my depression careened out of control. My husband, Larry, and I had just celebrated our seventh anniversary, but it wasn't a happy occasion.

"Larry, why do you work so many hours?" I unwisely asked again. "Having a two-year-old and a newborn is hard work. I need you to help me."

"Kathy, I try to help you," said Larry. "Being a policeman is demanding. I'm working all those hours to secure our financial future."

I knew I'd spoiled our time together. Silence surrounded us and a fog of hopelessness encircled me. My thoughts turned inward. *Kathy, you never do anything right. Larry hates you.*

Then in my own defense, I screamed inside, *I hate him too.*

Doubts and fear haunted me. *Will we get a divorce? Why can't we talk? We used to be in love.*

Then I prayed silently, *Lord, we're Christians. We're not supposed to be acting like this. What's wrong?*

I often prayed for God to heal my marriage and help me with my angry reactions to our two-year-old daughter. My anger toward Darcy escalated when I felt rejected by Larry. Her strong-willed nature resisted toilet training and resulted in constant temper tantrums that wore me down. I continually yelled at her. But soon my reactions deteriorated into angry spanking, kicking, and pushing. I felt totally powerless to stop my behavior.

"Oh God, help me!" I cried. When my rage increased and my prayers went unanswered, I concluded God had given up on me.

The day after our disastrous anniversary dinner, I caught Darcy playing in the fireplace ashes.

"Darcy!" I exploded. "How many times must I tell you not to play with the ashes in the fireplace?"

I ran over to her and screamed again and again as I choked her. In my frenzy, it was as if I left my body and was outside myself, watching a horrible movie scene of a crazed woman choking a little, blonde-headed toddler.

Then within seconds, I was back in my right mind. I jerked my hands away from Darcy's throat. She gasped for air and began shrieking. I ran down the hall, trying to escape the horrible scene. "Oh, God, I don't deserve to live."

I slammed my bedroom door behind me. *I'm a terrible mother. I can't believe I did that.*

Then I remembered what Larry had said before he left for work. "Kathy, I'm leaving my off-duty service revolver in the top dresser drawer today because I don't need it. Don't let Darcy get close to it."

"That's the answer—Larry's gun," I said to myself.

A tiny voice in my head sinisterly whispered: *Take your life. God doesn't care. Otherwise He would instantaneously deliver you from your anger and heal your marriage. There's nothing for you to live for.*

With trembling hands, I opened the top dresser drawer, and the gleam from the shiny barrel of the gun invitingly glinted at me. Darcy's crying from the other room wrenched my heart. *She's better off without me. I've ruined her for life.*

I stared at the gun and began reaching into the drawer. But then a new thought suddenly entered my mind. *What will people think of Jesus if they hear that Kathy Miller has taken her own life?*

My hand stopped. The faces of the women in the neighborhood Bible study I led flitted before me. My family members who didn't know Christ rushed to mind. I thought of my unsaved neighbors whom I had witnessed to.

Oh, Lord, I don't care about my reputation, but I do care about Yours. I call myself a Christian, and so many people know it. What will they think about You if I use this gun?

The concern for Jesus' reputation saved my life that day, and I knew it was prompted by the Holy Spirit. At that point, I did not have any hope, but in the following months, God proved Himself faithful by revealing the underlying causes of my anger. He gave me patience to be a loving mom. Overtime, He healed my relationship with Larry.

Suddenly, my reverie snapped back to the present as the train began slowing down for the next stop. I looked over at Darcy, who had awakened and was gazing out the window. I smiled.

The thought forcefully struck me: *If I had taken my life, I would have missed Darcy's wedding three years ago and our son's graduation from college. I wouldn't have had the opportunities to speak in 30 states and seven foreign countries or to write 49 books.* The list went on and on. I thought of Larry, who is my best friend, and of our 35 years of marriage. If I'd used the gun that day, Larry probably would have remarried. And I knew my daughter and son would have grieved over a missing mother who seemed to be more absorbed in her own pain than about their welfare.

Yes, I understood how Greg could have so little hope that he took his own life. But I wish I could have shared with him that there is always hope. God is faithful if we continue praying and holding onto His promises. I'm so grateful I did.

Darcy's voice pulled me back into the present.

"Mom," she said, turning to me. "I'm so excited we're spending a vacation together in New York City."

"Why are you cast down, O my soul, and why are you in turmoil within me? Hope in God; for I shall again praise Him, my salvation and my God."
Psalm 42:11 (ESV)

———

Kathy Collar Miller is the author of 49 books including *Partly Cloudy with Scattered Worries*. She is a popular women's conference speaker who has spoken in 30 states and seven foreign countries. Visit her at www.KathyCollardMiller.blogspot.com.

35

Secrets No More
John Warton

My wife and I have four children. All of them are grown, more or less, but our youngest has always been the most willful. She is a strong, brave girl, and self-reliant to a fault. Despite a youth that was full of teaching and the example of her elder siblings, she began to live on her own with a boyfriend. And it should have been no surprise that she did not want us to know where.

We knew she was somewhere on the other side of the city, but our only contact was an occasional cell phone call that she would initiate when she had some credit on it. After months of praying, refused invitations, and no contact with her, I finally came to a point of desperation. I could not tolerate this any longer.

Rather than filing a missing person report with the police, hiring a private investigator, or roaming the streets of the city—hoping to see her, her car, or her childhood dog, Annie—I decided to seek help by praying that God would reconnect us.

I approached two groups of men in my church: the elder board, of which I was a member, and my small group that met each week. It may sound as if confessing to these men the fact I did not even know where my daughter was living required considerable humility, but it did not. I simply wanted to find her. I explained the situation to both groups and asked them to pray with my wife and I that God would allow us to make contact with her.

To the best of our ability, we mixed this prayer with faith and submission. We believed that God could make this happen in a moment—or disallow it as part of His larger plans for her or us. We asked specifically and "in His Name," according to John 14:13.

And nothing happened. A week went by, and there was no impromptu visit or phone call. We prayed on. Then Saturday evening of the second week, my wife and I had finished dinner and were about to start a movie when the phone rang. The call was from a local number that we did not recognize. Nonetheless, I answered.

A middle-aged woman was on the other line, asking if we owned a dog named Annie. I informed the woman that Annie was our dog, but our daughter was keeping her now. Apparently Annie had wandered into her yard. When the woman brought her inside, she found the nametag that listed our phone number.

After taking the woman's phone and address, I called our daughter. She didn't answer. After leaving a voice message saying that Annie had wandered away but I knew where to find her, I called our daughter's boyfriend who was working nights in a pizzeria. Somehow in the noise of the shop and all the activity, he heard the ring and had the time to answer. I relayed the same message that Annie had wandered away but I knew where to find her, and he promised to call our daughter.

It was just moments later when my wife felt we should go retrieve Annie ourselves. So I called the woman to tell her we were coming. After a drive across town, Annie's happy bark and jump assured the kind lady that we were indeed her owners. But before we could drive away, my phone rang. It was our daughter.

She told us she was out with friends looking for Annie on foot and was so thankful for my call. Then I told her that her mom and I had actually picked Annie up and had her in our car. She was effusive in her gratitude and told us the intersection she was at, which was just two blocks away.

Thirty seconds later, we were together, hugging, crying, laughing, and playing with a very happy dog. There were apologies for being so reclusive, promises of being together, and invitations to dinner at the house where she was staying.

Within two weeks, God had not only answered the specific request I had made, but had done so in a much larger way than my wife and I had ever imagined. We were able to reconnect with our daughter in a way that showed our concern for what was really important to her: Annie. Nothing, not even her boyfriend at the time, was as important to her as Annie. God gave us the opportunity to reconnect in a context of caring for the most important thing in her world.

Moreover, God had done a work in our daughter's heart so that she recognized her offenses to her parents and was truly sorry. The love we had for each other was reaffirmed. It was a beautiful moment. And more than just making phone connection or learning where she lived, we were face-to-face and reunited in heart. It was all a gift of God, an answer to prayer, and something we could not have engineered ourselves even if we had spotted her car in a driveway or received a report identifying her whereabouts.

To my surprise, this was just the beginning of God's answer to those prayers. In the next months, we did reconnect with our daughter on a regular basis. In discussions over meals, we learned for the first time some of the justifications she felt for turning her back on Christian values. When she became pregnant, we were allowed to help her. Before the birth of her baby, we were able to assist her and her boyfriend in obtaining their own house. And two years later, he asked our permission to marry her. Our families gathered for a Christian wedding that we always remember with joy.

To Thee, Oh Lord, we give thanks.

"And I will do whatever you ask in my name,
so that the Father may be glorified in the Son."
John 14:13

———

36

The Wild Pig
Mercy Ciniraj

My grandmother, Eliyamma Mathai, grew up in a heavily forested area in the Indian state of Kerala. Her family was religious, but had not been taught about what it means to have a living relationship with Jesus Christ. Child marriage was common in India at the time, so at the age of 13, she married a man named Mathai from the same religion.

Eliyamma and Mathai lived with her family in their mud house in the forest where they had no electricity or running water, and no local market to buy food. Her father and Mathai worked hard to reclaim the forest for their small farm, where they also cultivated coffee and spices such as pepper and cardamom.

Because they had no pipes to get suitable drinking water to their house, nor even a well nearby, it was part of the women's daily chores to fetch water from the river.

One day, when Eliyamma was 27 years old, she walked down to the river to fill up her water pot. As she bent over the water's edge with her pot, a wild pig charged out of the underbrush and brutally attacked her. She fought back, using the water pot as a defensive shield and weapon to swing at the head of the pig.

But as she fought, the wild pig became even more enraged and fierce. His sharp teeth ripped at her legs and arms. Eliyamma knew her life was in jeopardy when blood began to flow profusely from her torn body. She cried out for help, but no one was nearby.

Suddenly a man appeared out of nowhere. He drove the pig away, and then knelt down beside Eliyamma to attend to her wounds. When his hands touched the torn places on her body, she was immediately healed.

Still in shock, Eliyamma's eyes grew wide with astonishment as she saw the palms of the man's hands. They were nail-scarred: He carried the markings of crucifixion.

Reverence and awe filled Eliyamma's heart. Only one response came to mind as she recognized who attended her. She prostrated herself on the ground and said, "My Lord and my God!"

It was for but a moment that she was facedown in the soil, which was damp with river water and mingled with her blood. When she slowly raised her head, her Rescuer had disappeared.

After this dramatic incident, Eliyamma had an insatiable hunger to know more about Jesus. She accepted Him as her personal Savior, and as a result of her testimony, her entire family believed and received Jesus Christ as their Lord and Savior.

In their lifetimes, Eilyamma and Mathai had a total of 67 children, grandchildren, and great-grandchildren.

Being one of them, I grew up knowing Jesus as my Lord and Savior, and married a man named Paul who, though Muslim by birth, accepted Jesus Christ as his personal Savior and Lord on his twenty-first birthday while he was studying in university. Now we are winning souls for Christ.

My grandfather, Mathai, went home to be with the Lord when Eliyamma was 62. Thirty-nine years later, Jesus took Eliyamma home when she was 101 years old. Up until that day, she eagerly awaited being with her Rescuer face-to-face, and devoted her life to studying the Bible, praying for others, and glorifying her Lord as a living witness.

"The Lord is my light and my salvation—whom shall I fear?"
Psalm 27:1

Mercy Ciniraj and her husband Paul live in India. Together they serve in a ministry that is committed to bringing the Gospel of Jesus Christ to India and the Third World.

37

Wanting What He Wants
Linda Highman

"You've never had a date? Why not?"

I was an 18-year-old college freshman when that infuriating question was first asked of me.

"No one ever asked me out," I replied. *The answer's obvious: dating is a two-way proposition, after all. And as they say, it takes two to tango.*

The looks of pity on my roommates' faces, however, were only the beginning of their efforts to make me over. They began by plucking my eyebrows and teaching me how to style my hair. It didn't get me a date the next day, but I certainly felt better about myself.

Only God knows, but perhaps their efforts did eventually pay off. A group of choir members began to have lunch together. Per usual, the group was mostly girls; but it often included one friendly, non-threatening fellow with a sweet, tenor voice. At first we were "just friends," but then we became "campus brother and sister."

Finally, one Saturday night while standing on a chair cleaning my closet, I turned to my best friend with the confession, "I love him." I'd never said that before. Startled, I stopped for a few seconds of serious consideration; and then I confirmed the fact, "I love him!"

I immediately had questions. And they would continue for the next two and a half years. *How does he feel about me? What kind of relationship do we* really *have? Is this what God* really *wants for me? Is this His best for me—His plan for me?*

The tension built by these questions distracted me from my studies and drove me to play the dating games that had always disgusted me. However, my daily devotional—a habit begun when I was 11 years old— kept me grounded throughout this time.

The Christian university I attended reserved one room on each dormitory floor as the prayer room. It was available 24/7 for anyone who needed a quiet place to pray and meditate. I was there every morning on my knees, asking God for guidance for my life.

One day during my Bible reading, I was struck by Psalm 37:4: "Delight yourself in the Lord, and He shall give you the desires of your heart." I memorized it in a moment. At first I thought it meant that God would grant me what I wanted. But what did I really want? Did I really want the boy? Was he really "the one"? I found myself praying, "Lord, I *want* to want what you *want* me to want."

Gradually, I realized the true meaning of the verse. As I put God first in my life and made Him the center of my heart, He would put His desires there. God doesn't *grant* or *fulfill* our desires just because we read His Word every day. Rather, He gives the very desires themselves to fire our imagination and motivate us to follow the big plans that He has for each of us to accomplish.

In that quiet prayer room, as I learned to pray for *God's* desires to be mine and for His perfect will to be accomplished, the events of my romance played out. Eventually, in God's timing, I married the sweet tenor and we began our saga of shared careers, life's disappointments, and God's abundant joys. Through it all, the echoes of Psalm 37:4 have sustained and guided me.

"Delight yourself in the Lord, and He shall give
you the desires of your heart."
Psalm 37:4 (NKJV)

———

The Highmans were colleagues for 42 years as they taught in Oregon Christian schools. They continue in education as volunteers and tutors.

38

The Journey
Suzanne Frey

I am a big believer in having dreams and goals in life. However, I know a young man who had a dream, and I wanted to do everything in my power to stop it.

This man is Stephen, my first-born. As a child, he got along well with his sisters. He was responsible, always on the honor roll, trustworthy, and never really did anything substantially wrong. He even received a $42,000 scholarship to a private university in his senior year of high school.

But before going to college, Stephen wanted to go abroad and see more of the world. He wanted to understand how people lived outside of our hometown in Oregon. So he planned a way to take a gap year and travel internationally, using little resources and not always having a reliable itinerary.

I was so frightened at first, because not only did he want to travel internationally, but he also wanted to do it alone. But when your son is 19 years old and six-foot-five, he really can do anything he wants.

After pleading with him not to go, I tried to reason him out of it. After telling him all the reasons why I didn't want him to go, he did not change his mind.

Stephen left for his journey on the first day of that year.

Five minutes after saying a teary good-bye, I called a dear friend and told her what he had done.

"You are going to have a story too," she said. "Ask God to give you a promise from the Bible every day and journal what He shows you."

That day, God gave me this promise from Psalm 32:8: "I will instruct you and teach you the way you should go. I will counsel you and watch over you."

This verse became my prayer for Stephen over and over again. I prayed that God would instruct and teach him the way he should go, and that He would counsel and watch over him.

That evening I journaled: *Today, I realize that for the past 19 years, my life has been nurturing this boy. Protecting, helping, teaching, encouraging, challenging, stretching, paying for and praying for, feeding, guiding, and loving him. And now, Lord, you are his mother and his father. You will be the One to parent him because he is 100 percent out of my hands.*

When I woke up the next morning and realized this was not a nightmare but reality, I became fearful again. Then I opened my Bible, and found the promise in Isaiah 41:10: "So do not fear, for I am with you. Do not anxiously look about you, for I am your God. I will strengthen you and help you. I will uphold you with my righteous right hand."

I remembered something I heard a few months before: more than any other command in the Bible, God says, "Do not be afraid." It's what the angels told the shepherds. It's what Gabriel told Mary when he appeared to her and she was going to have Jesus. Things didn't quite go the way she had planned, either.

Yet each day God gave me an encouraging word.

Even when I was most afraid, God gave me a supernatural peace that couldn't be explained.

Meanwhile, I told my family, friends, and Moms In Prayer group about Stephen's journey. They encouraged me to send out regular emails sharing what I knew of his travels and the Scriptures God was leading me to pray, so they could pray with me. Soon Stephen had over 50 families praying for him.

I concluded from Psalm 139, wherever Stephen was, God was with him. Even when Stephen was far, far away, God's hand guided him and His right hand held him fast.

Day by day, and week by week, God answered specific prayers: from preserving his health while traveling through several foreign countries, to providing extra resources that enabled him to continue his journey.

Stephen returned home to our family in late August, after traveling almost nine months over 7,000 miles. He accomplished what he'd set out to do, and we eventually felt so proud of him for the courage and faith he had to take this adventure. To say it was good to have him home is an understatement.

Even though most people, including me, told him not to, Stephen followed his dream. Three weeks later he began classes at his new university. Later he graduated with honors.

I went on a journey as well. I went from being full of fear to being full of faith. God spoke to me in promises. He led me by His Word. As I asked Him to direct, protect, and provide for Stephen, He did.

Every day of the journey, I had a choice. Instead of dwelling on my feelings of fear, I learned to think about what I believed to be true: that when God makes a promise, I can count on it.

"I will instruct you and teach you the way you should go.
I will counsel you and watch over you."
Psalm 32:8

39

A Child's Prayer
Ginny Mooney

The year was 1977, and I was 10 years old. We had just buried my Uncle Al a week earlier. It had been my first funeral. We children sat off to the side in a section partially cordoned off with a curtain, so that we could hear the service but not see the body—my uncle's body.

Just a few days ago, Uncle Al had been perfectly fine, at least on the outside. He had gone into the hospital for open-heart surgery, but he never came out. My Aunt Evie, whose birthday I share, was inconsolable by the loss. They had met and married when she was 50. It was her first marriage and they had only five years together. She wailed over and over again, "How could this happen?"

She stood in the parking lot of the funeral home sobbing, refusing to go in. My father tried to console her weeping form, and in that moment, something happened—Aunt Evie said God touched her and a wave of complete peace descended on her. After that, it seemed everything would be okay.

One week after the funeral, I came home from school to find my mother worried and upset. She explained my Dad had gone in for his yearly check-up and they found something wrong with his heart—a blockage.

A blockage? Thought my 10-year-old self. Panic raced through me. *What did that mean?*

My mom gently explained to me that a blockage means blood can't flow to and from the heart freely. It was fairly large, they thought, and they might have to operate. But before they did that, they would do one more test to measure the exact size and to confirm its location. This procedure was called a catheterization. The word was big and scary, but it wasn't as scary to me as the word "operate." I knew an operation meant surgery. Wasn't it heart surgery that my Uncle Al had just undergone and not survived? I was thunderstruck. *My father could die. Die! How would I ever survive?*

My dad was more than just my father; he was my hero. Every day after school, my sister, brother, and I watched for him to come home from work and ran to the door to meet him, climbing on him like a jungle gym. My dad was kind and gentle. He made us laugh. He loved people and they loved him. He rarely passed my mom or us children in the house without giving us a kiss on the cheek or a little squeeze. Even when my dad worked late, he would come home and check my homework for the next day. I didn't just love Dad; I adored him.

Now he might go away, just like Uncle Al.

As I thought things over in my 10-year-old heart, I knew there was only one person who could save my father. I went quietly to my room and got down on my knees by my bed, as I had seen my father do every night for as long as I could remember. I clasped my hands, looked up, and spoke to God: "Lord, please, please, please don't take my father away. Please! I love him so much and we all need him. Mom needs him, I need him, and Jennifer and John need him. Please, Lord, heal him if You can. But please don't take him away."

I didn't stop praying. I pleaded with God over and again, every day, up to the day of his test. Sometimes as I prayed, I thought about the way God had answered my Aunt Evie's prayers for help by reaching down and comforting her so she could go on after Uncle Al's death. It was a good answer, but it was not the kind of answer I wanted from God. Not at all!

The day came for my dad's test. As we left for school, Dad and Mom tried to assure us all that everything would be okay. I nodded and smiled, not wanting them to see my fear. They had enough to worry about.

I went to school that day and kept praying through classes, lunch, and recess. I had heard that God always answered prayers. But what kind of answer would it be?

I raced into the house after school and my mom came to greet me, smiling. Maybe the blockage wasn't as big as they thought. Maybe they wouldn't have to do surgery at all, or maybe it could wait a while.

"You'll never believe what happened, Ginny," my mom said as we sat on the couch together. "The doctors went in with the catheter and they couldn't find the blockage. They couldn't find any blockage. It was completely gone! They didn't know what to think. They were completely amazed." And then she added with a smile, "Daddy's heart is just fine."

The doctors may not know what to think, but I did! I hugged my mom tight and then ran to my room and got back down on my knees. I looked up with a giant smile on my face, even as I tasted the salt of tears. "Thank you, God, thank you," I said over and over again. "Thank you for giving me my Dad back!"

Since that day, over 35 years ago, there have been many times God has answered my prayers in ways other than what I wanted. Sometimes He has said "no" or "not now." Pastors' tell us He is teaching us patience or trust when He does that. I am sure they are right.

But on one glorious day in 1977, God said a big "yes!" to a little girl's anxious prayers. He knew I needed my Daddy. And that is an act of another Father's love I will never forget.

"So if you sinful people know how to give good gifts to your children, how much more will your heavenly Father give good gifts to those who ask Him."
Matthew 7:11 (NLT)

———

Ginny Mooney is a freelance writer and Emmy Award-winning television producer. She lives in Florida with her two children, Azalea and Asher.

40

Time for a New Terry
Judy Neibling

"Don't you do what Ginny did," my brother Terry angrily warned me.

It was the mid-70's. We were at our parents' home in Maryland, talking about giving our hearts to Jesus, which our older sister, Ginny, had recently done.

I was 19 years old, and I was thinking about giving my heart to Jesus, too—but I was far from telling Terry that. He was the big brother I fought with growing up, but dearly loved. I understood where he was coming from: all three of us siblings grew up going to church every Sunday, but none of us had been close to God. A year after Ginny shared her newfound peace and joy with Terry and me, I began to do the same with him. But he thought it was all a "bad idea."

Soon afterwards, Terry's infant daughter died, and his marriage crumbled. He left Maryland for Wyoming and started a new life there. Meanwhile, Ginny and her husband, Dan, joyfully decided to pack their bags and become missionaries in Papua New Guinea with Wycliffe Bible Translators. Then God called me to become a staff member for Campus Crusade for Christ—now called Cru. I served in the U.S. Virgin Islands, Mexico, and then, after meeting my husband, Ed, in the Philippines.

The four of us started praying for our Terry.

I had heard of fasting as a young believer, so I decided to fast and pray one meal a week for Terry's salvation. I usually fasted lunch on Friday, unless I was pregnant or nursing one of our three children.

Sometimes my prayers were impassioned, but more often than not, they felt feeble. Nonetheless, the habit of fasting reminded me to pray.

Whenever Ed and I visited the United States, it was difficult to figure out what to talk about with Terry. We had very little in common. He was either working in the oil fields of Wyoming or driving across the country in trailer rigs. Every few years, I would write to him about giving his heart to Jesus. He never seemed interested, but in 1985 I wrote in my journal that Terry had told me "I'm not a heathen," and that knowing Jesus "sounds good." The same journal entry included my study of Romans 10:1, where the Apostle Paul wrote: "My heart's desire and my prayer to God for the Jews is for their salvation." I wrote: "Is my brother's salvation my dearest dream? Yes—and my prayer."

Four years later, I heard Joy Dawson of Youth With A Mission speak at a conference in Manila, Philippines. She recommended that we pray not only for the salvation of our loved ones, but also that they would become Christians of influence. I added that to my prayers for Terry.

Then, while driving a truck through Florida in 1996, Terry looked for a radio station to tune in to, but could only find a Christian one. As he listened, the speaker said something that led Terry to conclude that Christianity might be true.

Not long afterwards, Ginny, Dan, Ed, and I were on furlough from our mission work, and we decided to meet in Kansas, where Ed is from. Ginny was celebrating her fiftieth birthday while we were there, and Terry flew in as a surprise. He had magazines to show us what he had ordered from that Christian radio station. Then, one night during our visit, he had a dream that I was standing on the other side of an open door, calling to him to come through.

The next evening after dinner, each of us shared again with Terry how we came to know Jesus. Dan asked Terry what he thought salvation would be like, and he answered, "It's like going through a door." We all agreed. Terry did not tell us he answered that way because of the dream he had had the night before.

We thought he might pray with us and put his faith in Christ at the table that night, but he did not. Ed asked him if he knew what to do if he wanted to begin following Christ, and he said he did.

On the phone with Terry a few days later, I heard the news I longed to hear for 21 years. Alone in his cabin out on the plains, Terry had prayed: "My Father in heaven, please forgive my sins. Thank you for your Son dying on the cross. Please come into my heart and be my Lord and Savior."

"Immediately, spiritual things started happening," Terry now recalls. He's never said what those things were—we only know that a spiritual transaction took place. Our joyful, peaceful brother became proof of 2 Corinthians 5:17: "Therefore, if anyone is in Christ, he is a new creation; old things have passed away, and look, new things have come."

Whenever we talked with Terry before he came to know Christ, we were at a loss for words. Now, he has a Bible verse or doctrine in mind to discuss as soon as we start talking. Our animated conversations can go on for hours. He studies Scripture with others and earnestly ministers in the local prison with his church. He loves to pray and tell co-workers, friends, and strangers how they can know Jesus—he has become a Christian of influence!

Twenty-one years of prayer and 17 years of fasting one meal a week—how it all seems like nothing now that Terry knows Jesus. Having this "new" brother is one of the greatest answers to prayer in my life.

"Therefore, if anyone is in Christ, he is a new creation; old things have passed away, and look, new things have come."
2 Corinthians 5:17 (HCSB)

———

Judy and her husband, Ed, are missionaries with Cru.

41

Do Not Worry

Deb Meyers

It was the week before Christmas when we got the call: my husband Ed was diagnosed with cancer.

Even though we knew his form of cancer was slow growing and treatable, I was gripped with fear and anxiety. My first instinct was to reach out to family and friends to ask for prayer. However, my husband wanted to wait until after the holidays to tell anyone, to give him time to digest the news, research treatment options, and meet with specialists. It would end up taking several months for all this to happen.

Satan does some of his best work when we feel isolated. I felt paralyzed by fear, wondering: What if he dies? What will my life be like without him?"

But God was speaking.

I received a little devotional book for Christmas, which I began to read. After the New Year, several small group Bible studies picked up again. It was uncanny that in both the devotional book and each of the Bible studies, the focal Scripture passages were all centered around God's commands: do not worry, do not fear, and trust Me.

These messages started coming on a weekly basis—it seemed like everywhere I went, God was telling me: "Do not worry, do not fear, and trust Me."

Then they started coming even more frequently as the weeks turned into months and we grew closer to having to make decisions about my husband's treatment.

I shared these God-incidences with my husband each time they happened. We took courage in them. But sooner or later, I found fear creeping back into my mind.

One day, I received a phone call from one of my closest faith sisters.

"I know this is going to sound strange," she said, "but you keep popping into my mind. I keep hearing the words, 'Don't be worried or afraid.' I feel weird about calling you, but is there something going on that I don't know of and about which you should stop worrying?"

I didn't know whether to laugh or cry.

"Yes, something is going on, but I can't tell you about it yet," I replied. "But God has been sending me this message quite often lately, and He is apparently using you today to deliver it. I will tell you more as soon as I can, but in the meantime, keep Ed and I in your prayers. God knows what it's all about."

I hung up the phone and called my husband to tell him this latest "do not worry" message. As we both chuckled, I realized that the time had come: I needed to start taking God at His Word!

It was time to put my faith into action and fully trust that God was walking with us and would provide the strength we needed to face this trial, regardless of the outcome.

My husband and I had been praying for four specific things: that God would guide us to the right specialist, help us choose the best treatment, minimize the treatment's side effects, and grant total healing.

After learning that my husband was a good candidate for all available treatment options, we decided to talk to a world-class surgeon and radiation oncologist. My husband felt leery about surgery because of its risk factors, and the surgeon spoke of his patients like they were statistics. In contrast, my husband felt instant rapport with the radiation oncologist. Thus, the best form of radiation treatment quickly became obvious and our initial prayers for guidance were answered.

After two months, and with a plan finally in place, we were at last prepared to talk with friends and family and ask for their prayers.

It was hard, facing the reality that I had very little control over anything in this situation. But that led me to turn to God for comfort and strength, and to gratefully accept the love and support of our community. As we continued to lean into God's words—do not worry, do not fear, and trust Me—we found ourselves living more fully in the present moment.

A gift received from going through cancer with my husband is that we learned to cherish each day; to tell others how much we loved them and why they are so important to us. We learned to slow down and savor the beauty of a sunset, and the first buds of spring. We found ourselves seeing with fresh eyes what is truly important in life, while what is superficial and unimportant became readily apparent.

We took a walk one day, holding hands and laughing at the antics of our dog. Suddenly I realized how many moments of joy we were experiencing in the midst of these difficult circumstances.

Although the cancer was still there, God was transforming the way I thought about and responded to it. I was learning to trust in the reality and presence of God in my daily life, His ability to guide, strengthen, and speak to me through His Word, prayer, and friends of faith.

When the day of treatment finally arrived, a sense of calm came over me. A friend came and sat with me during the procedure and we prayed that God would guide Ed's medical team. We prayed that the treatment would kill all cancer cells and that Ed would experience minimum side effects. We gave thanks for the availability of world-class health care and for health insurance. We gave thanks for the knowledge that God was with us and had walked before us.

The procedure was supposed to take two hours. It took four. During that wait I repeated the words: "Do not worry, do not be afraid, I am with you always." And in those moments, trusting by faith in God's promises, I felt His Spirit calm my heart and grant me peace.

I never sensed that the "do not worry" message was about God promising miraculous healing. It was a message about trusting in God's faithfulness to be present with us—regardless of the outcome.

Nearly two years have passed since that day; I thank God that Ed's treatment has shown successful. He still experiences some side effects of treatment, which is to be expected. Although I don't think about the cancer on a regular basis, we continue to pray for Ed's continued healing.

I give thanks for the lessons in trust that God taught me through this process. Now I know that when new trials assail me, I can trust in God's presence and strength to see me through them. Because facing life's fears and worries is a daily battle, trusting in and surrendering to God is a daily choice. Only when I am surrendered do I experience peace in His presence. And it's because of the gift of His presence that I can more easily do as 1 Thessalonians 5:16-18 says: "Rejoice always, pray continually, give thanks in all circumstances; for this is God's will for you in Christ Jesus."

"The Lord Himself goes before you and will be with you; He will never leave you nor forsake you. Do not be afraid; do not be discouraged."
Deuteronomy 31:8

———

42

Hope for Tomorrow
Ron Marlette

Drugs and alcohol. I was 12 years old when these became my ways to escape the pain of life, family addictions, and homelessness. At the age of 14, I started dealing drugs and dropped out of school because it got in the way of my addiction. Over the next seven years, I fell deeper and deeper into the abyss of addiction and crime.

When I was 21 years old, the police came to visit me. As they were looking for my large stash of drugs, I was looking for a place to hide. They did not find what they were looking for, but they left me a note that read, "We'll be back." That note terrified me because I was dealing a high quantity of drugs! In that one moment, as I held that note in my shaking hands, I realized I needed to change my life.

With no hope in myself for recovery, I checked into a drug and alcohol recovery program, and decided to try for something that had alluded me for 10 years: live a clean and sober life. It didn't take long to realize this also meant staying away from the people, places, and things that were associated with my drug lifestyle. If I didn't, there would always be temptation toward my old ways.

Soon after being released from rehab, I ran into a friend who used to regularly invite me to church. I always thought she was crazy, considering she knew what kind of lifestyle I was living. This time she invited me to attend a Billy Graham Crusade. I decided to go. It was there, in that stadium, sitting among thousands of people, where I first heard a clear presentation of who Jesus was, how He saw me, and how He could help me live a life of peace, purpose, freedom, and hope.

Then and there, I asked Jesus to help me live the life that I could not—a life of faith, hope, and love. I started learning about living with compassion, mercy, and grace. I now knew that *by grace I was saved, through faith, that not of myself, but a gift of God*! I started a recovery support group at the church I was attending, passionately believing that if I could find victory over my addictions, I could help others, as well.

Sensing an overwhelming burden to do more, I went back to high school and received my diploma. Then I went to Multnomah University for my four-year degree, becoming the first person in my family to graduate from college. God continued to bless me with a wife, Jennifer, and we now have five grown children. Soon after graduation, I was asked to launch a satellite mission in Solano County, California to serve the homeless and addicted. Fifteen years later, Mission Solano's Bridge to Life Center stands as a testimony of God's faithfulness to His vision of showing grace, mercy, and compassion.

Many times over the years, those who come to Mission Solano have told me: "Ron, you don't know what it's like. You don't know how hard it is to change and get off drugs and live a clean and sober life." But I smile and say to them: "Oh, I think I know what it's like, and let me tell you what it will take. And if you're ready, you too can live a new life."

I share with them about how God's love found and met me where I was. He gave me the *hope and help* I needed to stay sober and clean my life up. Most importantly, He gave me the hope of a life in Him and a passion to help others. I share that God told me in 1 Corinthians 5:17: "Anyone who is in Christ is a new creation, the old has passed away, behold all has become new."

We know the hope of Jesus Christ at Mission Solano, and we want to share it. It starts with a hot meal, a clean bed, and a new start. Yes, I know what it's like and, better yet, I know in Whom to find the strength, freedom, and hope for tomorrow.

*"For it is by grace you have been saved, through faith—
and this is not from yourselves, it is the gift of God."*
Ephesians 2:8

———

Ron Marlette is the founding CEO of Mission Solano Rescue Mission. He has five grown children and a gorgeous wife of 30 years, Jennifer. Mission Solano was birthed from a donated bus in the county where Ron once lived a homeless lifestyle as a youth. It has grown to be the largest mission of its kind in Northern California. It has been called "The Rescue Mission of the Future" because of its public and private partnerships and holistic programs.

43

Take It To The Bank
Joyce Frey

One day I felt the Lord nudge me to stop by the bank to inquire about interest rates on a certificate of deposit (CD).

We had a rental house we had been trying to sell for three months, but the property had a huge drawback: it was on the corner of a very busy street. We spent thousands of dollars fixing it up, both on the inside and outside, and we were still spending hours each week maintaining the yard and watering the newly planted shrubs and flowers.

So for three months we prayed earnestly for God to send a buyer. Now it was just days away from the listing to expire and no one had shown any interest in it.

At the bank, the teller directed me to the manager, who turned out to be a friendly young man. When he asked me why I wanted information regarding a CD, I explained the situation about our house, and told him that as soon as it sold, we would be interested in directing some of the money into a CD saving plan.

"Where is the house located?" the manager asked.

I told him.

"My wife and I love that area," he said. "I would like to see your house."

The next day, he came to our house and was very impressed. And the busy street did not seem to bother him at all.

"I would like to bring my wife to see the house," he said. "If she likes it, we will buy it!"

We were overjoyed, and yet tried to be cautiously optimistic in case his wife was not as thrilled about it as he was. We prayed for God's perfect will to be done and waited expectantly for their answer.

The next day we got the call: "She likes the house. We want to buy it."

The listing expired the very same week the bank manager bought it; so we did not have to pay the realtor fee. We ended up not investing in a CD, but put the money in an annuity instead.

I realized that going inside the bank that day had nothing to do with CD, but that it was truly a nudge from the Lord and an answer to prayer for the sale of our house.

My husband likes to say that I sold the house, but we both know it was God. And He gets all the glory.

"Now to Him who is able to do exceedingly abundantly above all that we ask or think, according to the power that works in us, to Him be glory in the church by Christ Jesus to all generations."
Ephesians 3:20-21 (NKJV)

44

No Slings Attached
Dawn Jeske

My daughter, Hannah, was a cheerleader her sophomore year in high school. One day during a stunt, Hannah caught the full weight of the flyer.

Pop! She heard as the flyer landed in her arms. It was her left arm. We thought it would be fine in a few days, but three weeks later, it had become excruciatingly painful to even move.

We took her to her regular doctor. She couldn't figure it out. So she recommended we see a pediatric, and later, an adult orthopedic surgeon. We did, but they couldn't figure out the source of the pain, either. Then we went to a physiatrist, who provided no answers; and then to our city's professional basketball team's sport doctor, who did an experimental procedure on Hannah where he drew blood, then re-injected it into her area of pain. This didn't work either.

We did several rounds of physical therapy, including a technique where metal instruments were rubbed against the painful area. All these therapies were tremendously painful for her and solved nothing. In addition to having two CAT scans, she had three MRIs where needles injected dye into her body (she *hates* needles), plus a bone scan which required doctors to inject her body with radioactive dye to visualize all of her bones. We even saw a tumor specialist, just in case.

None of them found an answer for her pain. By now Hannah was sick of seeing doctors and did not want to look for an answer anymore because the therapies hurt so much. So she bore the pain and wore a sling on and off for over three years.

During this time she couldn't play sports in school or games in her youth group. People started saying she was making it up because no doctor could find anything wrong. After three years of pain, she started wondering if they were right—if she was only imagining the pain.

Hannah saw one last doctor who proposed she had a rare condition called chronic regional pain syndrome. Over time, her limb would get hot, swollen, and red. Then it would soften and deform.

"Sometimes, people even get an amputation," he said. Hannah asked for an exploratory surgery, but the doctors would not do it because they could not find *any* medical evidence of something being wrong.

Sometime later at a Bible study Hannah and I attended, I felt God tell me to ask the group to pray for Hannah. They did, fervently asking God to help us find an answer and to heal her.

The next day, I searched online for a professional in chronic pain syndrome. As I scrolled though dozens of names, I felt led to click on a certain physical therapist's website. It said he had 50 years of experience and read: "If you want to stop your pain at the source rather than just strengthening the surrounding muscle, we are the experts."

I called and explained Hannah's story to the receptionist.

"When can I bring her in?" I asked.

"That physical therapist is semi-retired," she said. "And right now, he's on an extended vacation in the San Juan Islands. Would you like to see his associate?"

"No," I said, knowing inside that I needed to pursue the physical therapist himself. "I want to see the man with 50 years of experience."

"I'll call him and let him know," she said.

An hour later I got a call from the San Juan Islands.

"Hello," said the therapist. "I am really interested in your daughter's case. Tell me more."

I told him everything.

"I think I know what's wrong with her," he said. As Hannah would leave for college in two weeks, he scheduled an appointment for the following week, and left his vacation early to meet with us.

Meanwhile, Hannah was exhausted from seeing doctors and had basically given up hope. Moreover, she didn't want miss a shift of work in order to make the appointment.

"I'm not going," she said to me. But I knew the Lord had steered me to find his website.

When I told her I would replace her wages, she agreed to go.

The night before this appointment, I attended a friend's birthday party and asked the group to pray for this upcoming appointment. There in the restaurant, they stopped the celebration and took turns individually praying for her for several minutes.

The next morning, Hannah, her father, and I found ourselves sitting in yet another waiting room. By this time, we had a one-inch stack of medical papers from the past three years of long appointments, endless research, painful treatments, and failed attempts to fix the pain. As we looked around, we noticed a Bible on the coffee table. I wondered if he was a believer. If he was, it made sense why I had felt so drawn to call him.

The physical therapist listened to her for an hour, and then began pointing out details about her arm that we had never seen before. It was as if he saw the interior workings of her arm in his mind.

After observing for a few minutes, he said to Hannah: "A tendon popped off your bone and tore. Scar tissue is rubbing against the bone, sliding back and forth like pulling a knot on a string of yarn through a needle. The way you hold yourself to protect your arm from pain is actually perpetuating it."

The therapist knew exactly what was mechanically wrong with her, and moreover, understood her pain.

"It hurts so bad that you want to cut your arm off," he said. When we reminded him she was leaving for college in two weeks, he said: "We'll have this taken care of before then."

We did not believe him because of all we had been through, but he took such a personal interest in her that we decided to trust him.

Hannah began the new treatments as he prescribed. He made his associate rearrange his schedule, so he could assist us. Every day over the next two weeks, the pain level decreased. Hannah was able to completely control the pain, making it completely go away if she did the exercises and movements she was supposed to do.

She was able to do the small things again, like pick up her backpack and no longer wear a sling just to walk around.

At the end of the two weeks, I went to the physical therapist to thank him. "God has given me this gift," he said. "I am so happy to be able to use that gift to help people." He was so humble and such a servant of the Lord. God truly answered the prayers of the women in Bible study and all the people at birthday party in orchestrating this appointment and putting us together with the person who could help her.

Hannah had to endure a lot of nasty things in hopes of finding healing. She is also a hard worker, so sometimes she felt as if she wasn't doing her part. She wasn't able to sleep well at night, so she would feel exhausted all the time. And there were many times when she was simply emotionally overwhelmed; it was draining to have the pain be a daily reality for three years.

But now, everything's changed! If her arm and shoulder ever hurt, she knows exactly what exercises to do to remedy the pain. Hannah has completed her second year of college and can do all the activities she used to do, and which she wanted to do for years as a theatre girl: carry costumes, lift heavy things, move props, hip-hop, and swing dance. She hasn't had to wear the sling again.

Although her healing was delayed, we as a family pondered the story of Lazarus. Jesus purposefully waited four extra days to go to Bethany, so we too chose to trust that God had a purpose in Hannah's injury and timing in its healing. Mary and Martha went from being desperate, hopeless, and exhausted to being filled with gratitude and wonder by God's mighty working in an instant.

We too rejoice and wonder in God's ability to take a seemingly hopeless situation, and, in His wisdom and mercy, bring us hope and Hannah back into a renewed, active, and normal life.

"And pray in the Spirit on all occasions with
all kinds of prayers and requests."
Ephesians 6:18

———

45

Dark Road Home
Michelle Winder

It was my final semester in college. I was 21 and my roommate's boyfriend, Kevin, gave me a job serving cocktails at the Old Spaghetti Factory. I didn't dare tell my parents I'd quit my engineering job so I could spend more time hanging out at the beach with my friends. Although I was a practicing Catholic at the time, I had a very distorted view of God and was sure He would punish me for making such a stupid choice.

But one of my closest friends constantly told me he was praying I would have a *personal relationship* with Jesus. I'd laugh, trying to hide the fact that I didn't *want* God to notice me. I was afraid of Him. That is until one balmy San Diego night.

It was only 10:00 p.m. and I had just finished my shift. I leaned against the old, solid wooden door of the restaurant. *Nothing.* It was thick, heavy wood, but tonight it seemed as though someone was pushing on it from the other side. I forced all of my 104 pounds of weight against it. It suddenly gave way and I tripped through the doorway, glancing down the long dark road as I caught my balance. A loud click behind me finalized my exit.

The air was heavy for a San Diego night. At the far end of the block, a single streetlight lit up my shiny white Ford Pinto. A chill ran up my spine. I thought I heard Kevin's voice in the distance, "I'm happy to walk you out." But glancing back, I realized it was just a memory from my first day on the job. I shook my head, reprimanding myself for the ridiculous notion of his voice running through my mind. A light breeze lifted the stench of stale urine to my nostrils. Vomit rose in the back of my throat.

I had always been able to defend myself, and anyone else who needed it. Walking down the side of the dark, empty street and nearing my Pinto, I remembered the time I punched a 12-year-old boy who was bullying my brother. His mom called my parents after he ran home crying. No dessert that night—pretty severe discipline for a four year old. I chuckled nervously and continued walking, the Pinto clearly in sight. Still, uneasiness crowded me, but I scolded myself for irrational fear.

Out of nowhere, a large image appeared from around the corner at the end of the block. *Not unusual for a Friday night downtown,* I thought. He slowly shuffled toward me with his hands in his pockets, watching the ground below him. My heart leaped and pounded against my eardrums. Electric hair pricked my scalp. Words echoed in my head. I imagined a voice saying, "Go back inside."

I watched the man, who didn't seem to notice me, and embedded his description in my memory: *white, six-foot-four, 230 pounds, Marine fade.* Beads of liquid oozed from nervous pores as I marched on, aware of each deliberate step.

The man proceeded down the street toward the old wooden door of the restaurant, never leaving the sidewalk nor glancing my way. Keeping my eyes on him, I slipped the keys from my purse and gripped the largest one tightly. High heels echoed in the silence as they methodically struck the black asphalt. I would not—could not—give in to irrational fear!

The moment we passed, I picked up my pace. With him now behind me, the pounding in my ears came to a sudden halt as I reached my Pinto and jammed my key into the lock. Immediately, I felt his dark presence behind me. His large, hot hand gripped my neck. *Swirling. Dizzy. Darkness. Black.*

I'm not sure how much time passed. I didn't know where I was or what had taken place. Slowly, as if waking from a dream, I saw my perpetrator before me with his hands in the air. He looked gripped with fear. His mouth was gaping, and his eyes were wide open, staring above my head.

I stood up—numb, disoriented, and confused. I was frozen in space and time. Refrigeration trucks buzzed all around me, echoing in the thick, rancid air. My shoes and purse had vanished. Nothing made sense.

Suddenly, I felt a warm hand on my bare shoulder, where my torn dress was held together by a seam. A deep voice behind me shouted, *"Run!"*

I weaved through the trucks, running toward the single light above the restaurant door, my bare feet unaware of the rocky pavement. I continued up the sharp asphalt to the old wooden door. Gripping the large iron handle, I tugged. The door gave way with ease, flinging wide. I glanced back. I didn't see the perpetrator. But beyond the streetlight stood a tall man dressed in bright white with a blue satin sash. He was holding a sword in his right hand. *And I knew.*

That night, over 30 years ago, I realized the God I feared actually *knew* me; He cared enough to intervene on my behalf. I still do not know what happened during the time I was unconscious, but I committed my life to Him on my way home, alone in the car. Over time and through multiple miracles, I have gained the ability to love, trust, and enjoy a personal relationship Him. More importantly, I have learned to accept His love for me. *No turning back.*

"For the Son of Man has come to save that which was lost."
Matthew 18:11 (NASB)

———

Michelle Winder is a Third Degree Black Belt and multiple assault survivor who has a passion for life and freedom. She is a certified World Martial Arts Instructor, personal safety coach and professional speaker.

46

Twelve Minutes

Faye P.

It was a rainy Saturday afternoon that called for a quick shopping trip to the mall with my friend, Tami, to buy a gift card. I stuck my iPhone into a pocket in my jacket as we walked to the outside information kiosk to find the location of the store.

As we stood at the kiosk talking to the clerk, a young man came very close to me for a few seconds. I joked about it then shrugged it off. It wasn't until after Tami and I were walking out of the store with the gift card that I reached into my jacket pocket and realized my iPhone was gone.

Now I knew a cell phone was replaceable, but the precious pictures of my granddaughter, and even her bite marks on the case of the cell-phone were not. The color drained from my face.

I started to panic, but Tami reassured me that I must have just dropped my iPhone in her car. But when we retraced our steps all the way back to her car and looked inside, we found no phone.

We came back into the mall through Macy's and asked a manager to call security, all the while fervently praying that an honest person would find it and turn it in. Then we retraced our steps back to the store—still, no phone. Throughout this time, Tami was calling my phone. On the third call, someone answered.

"Hello?" It was a security officer.

Tami and I looked to each other with shock and relief on our faces. My eyes got huge with tears. Then I did a jig right there in the mall, praising God. We didn't care who saw or heard us. God, my heavenly Papa, needed thanks right then and there.

Then we sprinted to the mall's security office to retrieve my grand-baby-bitten cell phone, and it was there after talking with security that we deduced it was the young man at the kiosk who had pick-pocketed my iPhone. The security officer used the term "apple picking." Upon realizing my phone was security locked, the thief threw it downstairs where a thoughtful little girl and her mom found it and turned it into a nearby store's manager, who then brought it to the security office.

All of this happened in a matter of 12 minutes. We needed to catch our breath, so we sat down.

Neither one of us were really surprised that God provided, but we were in awe as to how faithful God was that He answered our prayers so quickly. Even though my request seemed trivial in the grand scheme of life, Papa cared enough to handle something that mattered to me, even though it was just an iPhone.

With our God, no prayer is too big, and no prayer is too small.

"Praise be to the Lord, for he has heard my cry for mercy. The Lord is my strength and my shield; my heart trusts in Him, and He helps me. My heart leaps for joy, and with my song I praise Him."
Psalm 28:6-7

———

47

His Eye Is on Me

Judy L.

Twenty-two years into my marriage, my husband was admitted to the hospital with a malfunctioning liver. Unless God intervened, he was expected to die.

Alone in my bedroom, I cried out to God for my husband's healing. In that moment, God's presence surrounded me and I knew He was telling me that He was with me in my husband's illness. I thanked Him for coming, gave myself to Him, and told Him I would do whatever He wanted me to do—just as I had done in my first month of marriage.

You see, my husband was not the man I thought I knew. In our 22 years of marriage, he had demonstrated a will of iron in which he used fear to control our daughter and myself. It had resulted in our complete isolation from the body of Christ by the time of his hospitalization. My daughter and I were not allowed to attend any church for over four years, because according to him, no church was doctrinally sound enough to even be called a church. He was convinced that he was protecting us from going down a slippery slope of doctrinal error where we would surely make shipwreck of our souls.

I had cried out to God for His help—and He came. For twenty-two years, He gave me strength to serve, love, respect, and submit to my husband.

My husband came home from the hospital and was placed on hospice care. I had an overwhelming desire to pray for three things. Firstly, I prayed God would restore his mind a little every day. Secondly, I prayed He would completely heal his body. And lastly, I prayed that God would deliver him from his underlying fears, which had not only done great damage to our marriage and family, but had controlled him his entire life. Fear truly was the strongest death-grip on him.

God began to answer my first two requests. After a few days, I noticed little changes in his mental processes. Then his blood pressure went up. After two weeks, he came off of hospice care and had a stint placed in his liver. And after two months, his memory and strength returned.

So I prayed and hoped for God to answer my third request—healing for his underlying fears and troubled past. Despite two godly men trying to counsel him, he was silent and unwilling to communicate. Instead of humbling himself and being willing to take an honest look at his life, he insisted that he was fine and in no need of understanding of what had happened to him. Rather than moving forward, he pulled us back into the way life was before his illness—a life filled with fear, isolation, and control.

But everything had changed for me. God had made it clear that He wanted to deliver us from the fear we were living under. I took a stand to go forward with God, rather than backward into fear. My daughter and I began attending a church nearby, and I continued to pray and wait for God to do something.

One day I came home to find my husband changing the lock on our front door. He was taking control of what he perceived to be my rebellious stance. I knew I would not be allowed back into the house until I agreed to submit and obey.

Yet he did not realize that in his locking me out, God had opened wide His door to me. My daughter and I moved in with my sister. It was now God's turn to take control, but His control was full of love, provision, comfort, and hundreds of small and big ways of showing me His eye was on me.

The following Sunday, we attended my sister's church. During the service, we went forward for prayer. I told the young woman who came to pray for us that I had been locked out of my home—nothing more. I was amazed as the woman began to pray about specific things that had happened in our home those past few months.

"Mom, how did she know?" asked my daughter on the way home.

I could only answer: "The Spirit of God was praying through her."

Now at this time, I had been a Christian for 42 years. I was a seminary graduate. I had studied the doctrine of God. I knew and believed that God was everywhere and He knew everything, but as I experienced God's love in that moment, He became more than a doctrine to believe. He became real and personal. I knew beyond the shadow of a doubt that God had been with me in my house all these years, listening, watching, knowing and caring.

The next Sunday I attended my sister's church again. But this time, I asked God for a word from Him. I had never asked Him for such a thing, and didn't know what I was asking for when I prayed for it. Nonetheless, He answered my request.

Before the beginning of the sermon, the pastor stood and said: "God has a word for someone here to today. You've been isolated from the body of Christ and you've been going through the most difficult time in your life. God wants you to know the body of Christ is here for you."

I immediately began weeping at these words. God was giving me His promise of provision through His people.

Three months later and without a word, my husband filed for divorce. A year into the divorce proceedings, during a two-week period of time, I prayed every day: *God, show me how much you love me.*

One Sunday, I sat back down after the church service was over and a young man with Down Syndrome walked up to me. He asked me in the sweetest voice if he could pray for me.

"God, show this lady how much you love her. Amen." Then he said: "I saw you sitting here all alone. I know what it's like to be alone."

Again, God heard my prayers! He used this young man to show me that His eye was on me, and that He is creative and personal in how He shows His love.

Five years have passed since our divorce at the time of this writing. They have been the most difficult years of my life. I have yet to find sustainable work as being a homemaker, homeschooler, and violin teacher in our home during our marriage did not allow for a career.

But God has promised He does have a work for me to do. I've waited on God, knowing He is always working *good* things together for lovers of Him.

While I cannot say I sailed through this trial with robust faith and unfailing trust in God, I can—I must—say that He is faithful and His Word is true.

Doubts have assailed me at every turn, and at times I have been overcome with fear and anxiety, but I have learned to live by worshipping, praying, fasting, reading my Bible, and continually asking for help.

I've been living every day with God, knowing what matters most is that He loves me and His eye is on me.

"Nothing in all creation is hidden from God's sight."
Hebrews 4:13

———

48

A Dime In God's Pocket
Beki Duke

Y ou cannot out-give God. You cannot be too generous with Him. I have tried.

Jeff, my husband of 34 years, and I met at summer camp when we were in our early twenties and married eight months later. We had three kids in four years. We bought a dairy farm, adopted two more kids, and kept living life at a fast pace. I often found myself praying from Matthew 6:10: "Father, may your will be done in our lives as it is in Heaven."

Just when it felt like life was settling down and we could ride the waves for a while, God prompted Grandma Duke, Jeff's 63-year-old mom, and hardworking grandma of 24 grandkids, to consider purchasing the old, vacant Trout Lake K-12 school building to turn into a summer camp. And she wanted us to be in on it.

Always a dreamer, she began wondering: *how does one go about turning an old school into a summer camp?*

God and grit was her answer.

The next few months were filled with serious and strange conversations between Jeff and me: somehow our roles had temporarily reversed. While I felt ready to jump headlong into this life-changing purchase, certain that God wanted us to sell our dairy farm and partner with Grandma Duke in this endeavor, Jeff did everything to fight against it. He loved our dairy farm—the cows and country lifestyle—so he resolutely stood on the notion that we were never selling it.

Yet through a series of miracles and because of his love for God, he changed his mind. When a stranger approached him about buying a piece of our land that we thought would never sell, Jeff knew his dairy farming days were over. He was offered $140,000 for the land—exactly the price of purchasing the old school. Again, we were praying, "Father, Your will be done."

Never in my wildest dreams did I think we would waltz into a room of school board members with a meager $2,500 in earnest money, an offer so simple it looked as though a fifth-grader could have written it, and five land sale contingencies. But in 1996, that is exactly what we did. And just days later, we made the phone call to the board, saying: "We now have the cash to buy the building!"

We sold the coveted family dairy farm of 60-acres, including the 4-H animals that our kids dearly loved, and proudly, like a bunch of hillbillies, moved into an old and doomy-looking school building with all our junk and a 40-horse-power John Deere tractor.

The old home-economics room became our "home" because it had a sink, countertops, some cupboards and a place for a stove and refrigerator. By adding a carpet remnant, couches, table and chairs, and a few more furnishings, we did well turning it into a home. Our kids' friends either thought we were crazy or cool. What other kids had a gym, tennis court, multiple showers and bathrooms, and their bed in a classroom?

Building from the ground up, this fixer-upper of a school became more than a home; it developed into a simple yet significant Christian camp and retreat center: Camp Jonah, where "Kids laugh, hearts change, and God smiles."

The name "Jonah" came from us teasing Jeff during our initial weeks of debating whether to go forth with the purchase: "So, Jonah, are you on board yet, or are you going to jump ship again?" Jeff thought Tarshish looked so much better than Nineveh. We related with the truth in this book of the Bible: when Jonah followed God, his small obedience made a huge difference in the kingdom of God, even though the school, from time to time, was not so different than the lonely, ugly, and stinky belly of a fish.

These years of watching Camp Jonah grow into our dream—God's dream—have been beautiful and hard. Yet every time we have a need, God provides: when our commercial dishwasher broke down, a donor replaced it; when we asked God for a 4x4 crew cab pick-up, some friends drove in and handed us the keys to theirs; and as our bookkeeper saw an upcoming deficit of $18,000 in the forecast, a check came in the mail for that very amount. This has been our story since 1996. God's will is being done!

After 15 years of living in the home economics classroom, Jeff and I moved into a travel trailer. I realized we were getting older (having grandkids will do that to you), so I began to take comfort in the fact that Jeff and I owned the school property. I thought that if the road got too tough, or if we couldn't pay the bills, or if we just wanted to retire, we could sell everything.

But one day in 2010, God spoke to my "Jonah" husband as he was praying in his favorite prayer spot—our Jacuzzi. He felt a heavy sense that God was actually with him in the water, telling him that we were to donate the property to Jonah Ministries.

Now we had discussed this in the past, but had always quickly put it aside. *Of course God wouldn't have us donate the property,* we thought. A few days later, Jeff told me that he made a deal with God: if I brought a "certain topic" up with him within a week, we were meant to do something about it. My soul knew exactly what this "certain topic" was. I hesitated, knowing that if I said it, my earthly security would be gone.

"Is it about donating the building to Jonah?" I said with great hesitation.

After a few moments of both of us sitting in shock and silence, Jeff latched on to this like a pit bull. Within days, he had handed the title over to our board. Meanwhile, I felt sick. There I sat—we were now totally broke. We had no earthly treasure. Of course, our board worked out our salary. Meanwhile, I worked hard to put a smile on my face. I realized I had to accept this new adventure.

Thanks to Jeff's persistence and encouragement, the smile became real. I slowly began to realize that what God really wanted was simple obedience and for me to enjoy the peace that comes from simply saying "yes." All we were doing was giving back to God the title to property that had been His all along.

Camp Jonah now hosts over 2,500 people per year; more than 300 of which are campers, and more than 2,300 of which are retreat guests. We host hundreds of local people at no cost for community events, namely the Trout Lake Fair, church activities, youth groups, and supervised visits for foster children.

Finally, throughout the years, there were times my heart ached for a home of our own. We often prayed that we could somehow purchase the home next door, as having neighbors so close was very stressful at times when you're running a camp. Every time I felt the ache, I would quickly give over our living situation to the Lord. In wanting God's will in my life, a certain tried-and-true measure of trust has grown in His ability to provide.

In 2012, the property was suddenly put up for sale. Through generous donors, an amazing grant, and God's grace, Jeff and I now live in that beautiful, often-prayed-for, miracle home next door, which is owned by the camp. We often ask each other when we have to "check out" of our "presidential suite." The view from every northern window is of the majestic Mount Adams and the glorious Trout Creek. The noise from Jonah's campers makes us smile. The house full of staff, guests, and grandchildren, fills every nook and cranny of our hearts. Once again, our faithful Father stepped in and answered our prayer of many years in His way.

We got caught up in His wild dream and have been living in the middle of a miracle ever since. We've come to realize that doing the hardest thing is sometimes the easiest choice when our prayer remains, *May Your will be done.* We've become certain that simple surrender pleases Jesus, and that the blessing we're enjoying today is just a dime in God's pocket.

"Blessed are those who trust in the Lord and have made the Lord their hope and confidence. They are like trees planted along a riverbank whose roots reach deep into the water. Such trees are not bothered by the heat or worried by long months of drought. Their leaves stay green and they never stop producing fruit."
Jeremiah 17:7-10 (NLT)

Beki Duke is the co-founder and camp coordinator of Jonah Ministries, a Christian Camp in the state of Washington, where "Kids laugh, hearts change, and God smiles."

49

Love Always
Jacqueline B.

For nine months I was a single mother of my son, Zayne, before I met and fell in love with Dave. Dave and I married a year later, and he adopted Zayne as his own.

At the time, Dave was working hard toward his degree, so Zayne and I spent every day together, just the two of us. We'd go to parks, the zoo, and the Museum of Science every chance we got, talking, laughing, and playing together the whole time.

When Zayne was five years old, Dave and I started having children of our own, but those five years with Zayne had formed a special bond between us that would never be broken.

As he grew, our conversations changed and became about more complex things—like relationships. He seemed to have no problem telling me anything or asking for my advice. After he moved out, he still called me regularly to share an idea, talk about an event, or just to say, "I love you, Mom."

One day, he started talking about a woman he met at work, Paige, who was a single parent of a young son. Paige revealed to Zayne her fear that she would never find a man who would love her and her son.

But Zayne told her not to give up, as he too was the son of a single mom and his mom had met and married a wonderful man who became his father. And soon, Zayne's relationship with Paige began to blossom. He brought her over for dinner one night to meet us for the first time.

She was a beautiful woman with a kind demeanor, and we got along well.

When it appeared there might be a wedding in the near future, they told us that they were doing things in a less-than-ideal order and that a baby was on the way. They decided to become husband and wife before the birth of their child with only her parents and Dave and I as witnesses, and then hold a big, summer wedding after the baby arrived.

They had a beautiful baby girl, Emma. After she was born, I began feeling animosity from Paige, but I didn't know why. She would tell me that I wasn't holding Emma correctly. I made a comment that I had raised three children, held many babies in my lifetime, and never been told this before, but it seemed to make matters worse. When we arrived at the bridal shower before the summer wedding, Paige graciously hugged my mother-in-law and daughter, but turned her back to me. During the party, Emma was being passed around so all could admire her. But when she was finally put in my hands, Paige came over and took her out of my arms, saying she needed to change her. When she finished changing her, she passed her into someone else's arms. Every time I got close to Emma, Paige would snatch her away for another reason.

After that, I began steaming inside every time we were together. She avoided eye contact and only talked briefly if I spoke to her first. I was shocked at her treatment of me. I felt like my son had married an enemy—and she was now part of our family! Zayne's marriage to Paige began affecting my relationship with him. I felt angry, hurt, and sad.

Finally, the day of the summer wedding arrived and I was told not to hold the baby during the wedding. I felt terrible. I was supposed to be happy for Zayne, but instead a dark cloud hung over me because I was blaming Paige for her horrible treatment of me.

Now in the past, I would simply distance myself from people who treated me badly. But how could I even think to cut off my relationship with Paige, the woman whom my dear son Zayne was now married to and who was the mother of my granddaughter?

So I began to pray. I told my trusted friend all that had occurred between Paige and I, and we prayed about it together. Then, when I opened my Bible, God took me to Mark 10:7-8, which says: "Therefore a man shall leave his father and mother and hold fast to his wife, and the two shall become one flesh. So they are no longer two but one flesh."

In that moment, I remembered my love for Zayne. As a mother, neither he, nor the rest of my children, always acted wonderfully. But even when they were rebellious, sassy, and mischievous, and I in turn felt angry and disappointed, I still always had a love for them that went beyond their actions.

God showed me through this verse that if I loved Zayne that much, and if Paige and he were one flesh, then I was to love her, too.

After talking with Zayne and praying for wisdom in this situation, I began reaching out to Paige. And as I took steps of faith to make things right with her, our relationship was restored and transformed by God's love.

Since then, I have learned to ask for forgiveness and pursue making things right when we've had misunderstandings. I have been asked to babysit my grandchildren for evenings and weekends on a regular basis, and I am deeply involved in their lives.

In the thick of the emotions of feeling terrible and at a loss for what to do, I truly believed nothing could help. But I was wrong. God showed me that I could *love always*. And with Him, all things are possible.

"Love is patient, love is kind. It does not envy, it does not boast, it is not proud. It does not dishonor others, it is not self-seeking, it is not easily angered, it keeps no record of wrongs. Love does not delight in evil but rejoices with the truth. It always protects, always trusts, always hopes, always perseveres."
1 Corinthians 13:4-7

———

50

Miracle Awakening

Larry Poland

Remote is hardly a sufficient word to describe the tall forest jungles of Peru in South America.

It is so dense that only two months before I entered it, I heard a report that a Boeing 727 had crashed into its trees. It took a search party six weeks to find the wreckage, even though they knew the mile radius of where it went down. The trees had literally swallowed it. It took a commercial plane flight over the Andes jungle city of Pucallpa, a small plane flight into the heart of the jungles, and a half-day cruise on a riverboat to get about 50 other missionaries and me to Lake Tipishca. It was 75 miles from the nearest unpaved road.

The occasion that brought me this far off the unpaved road was an annual four-day retreat and planning session of missionaries from a Florida-based missionary organization, of which I was the main speaker. The missionaries had travelled there from a number of South American countries.

I spoke on the first day in the morning, and sensed that the spiritual climate was cold. Even the proximity to the Equator couldn't warm it. At first, the attendees were kind to each other, but then attending an afternoon business session revealed to me that a number of them had some pretty awful attitudes. One man suggested they shut down their mission efforts in more than one country. I watched as discouragement and despair filled the room.

Moreover, I witnessed strife within the families. I was graciously given a bedroom in one of three homes that had been built for the permanent missionary families assigned to the mission base and Bible school at Tipishca. Built crudely of native material, the home's thin walls could not prevent me from hearing the unkind way the husband spoke to his wife and daughters. It was awful. I nearly wept.

I called the heads of the mission together that evening and said that I thought we were wasting our time with the teaching sessions each morning. I shared my perspective that the spiritual climate was cold, the missionaries were just going through the motions, and my messages were falling on deaf ears. I recommend that we suspend the well-planned schedule and meet for a time of confession, prayer, and healing until God came down and met us.

The leaders were surprised at the suggestion. They had put a lot of effort into planning the conference. Nonetheless, they agreed to the plan. We spent time in prayer, asking God to do a special work in all of our lives. Then the head of the mission announced the suspension of the schedule indefinitely to the group.

The next morning, all 50 of us met in the largest room of the Bible school. I gave a short devotional from Ephesians 5, titled "The Holy Spirit and Interpersonal Relationships," slowly reading through the passage and highlighting how relationships controlled by the Spirit of Christ are marked by harmonious communication, praise, and thanks to God and mutual submission to each other. The message was not spectacular and the passage was surely not new to these veteran servants of Christ.

Then I announced we would be spending an indefinite period of time in prayer together, suggesting we begin with silent self-examination. Everyone bowed his or her head. After a few minutes of silence, I heard sniffling. It was a bit strange; it was as if an upper respiratory virus has suddenly broken out in the room. I looked up and people were weeping. I let the prayer and weeping continue.

"Now, I think it would be good to focus our prayer on confession," I said, quietly. "If anyone has anything to confess, please share it with us all."

After a few moments of pause, the wife of one of the three couples stationed at Tipishca stood and burst out: "Oh, God, forgive me! I have hated Eileen (I don't remember her real name). I have envied her talent..." And she broke down and wept aloud.

The room went silent, but the sniffing continued. Then the father of the home where I was staying stood and cried: "Oh, God, forgive me! I've been a *wretch* to my wife and daughters!" He sobbed his way out of his prayer.

What happened the rest of our time that morning defies verbal description. One after another, these dear missionaries stood and confessed their bad attitudes, rebellion toward leadership, lack of faith in tough circumstances and more. Not one of them had a dry eye; I was dabbing the tears running down my cheeks as well.

With this long session of confession now clearing their hearts, I felt a tug to launch a season of singing praises. It was incredible. With no instruments, one person after another launched a hymn, gospel song or chorus a cappella, and the room burst into the most passionate harmony. It was a Tipishca version of angel choirs—it was *heavenly*.

The morning passed so quickly. We were stunned when one of the leaders announced it was lunchtime.

So I suggested to the group: "Before you leave the room, give someone a hug and make anything right with them that needs to be resolved."

I will never forget what I saw next. The woman who had confessed her hatred for the other woman had embarrassed her, wept on each other's shoulders. A burly missionary approached an executive from the headquarters office in Florida, lifted him off the floor in a bear hug and confessed: "I've hated everything that comes out of that office; that is wrong. Please forgive me!" They wept with each other.

Filing to the next building for lunch was an exercise in spiritual buoyance. The laughter and interaction was light and joyful. But there was one dimension I did not expect and had never witnessed before. In the New Testament book Acts 2:44-45, describes a scene in which the Holy Spirit fell on those gathered on the day of Pentecost: "And all those who had believed were together and had all things in common;

and they began selling their property and possessions and were sharing them with all, as anyone might have need." This historical and miraculous event is a stunner: God supernaturally worked in their hearts and *willingly* separated them from ownership of their most prized possessions.

It started happening in the lunch line. A missionary noticed his friend shooting pictures and commented that his camera looked new. The man shooting the photos described the features of his brand new camera, and then lifted it off his neck to give to his friend.

"No, no," the friend protested. "I have a good camera." Arguing that this new camera was better than his, the man made another attempt to get him to keep it.

I saw one woman admire a necklace with fabulous beadwork that another woman was wearing.

"Where did you get that beautiful necklace?" she asked.

"The women in the village in my Bible study made it for me and gave it to me as a present," she replied.

"Here, I'd like for you to have it." Over her protests, she lifted the necklace over her head and placed it around her friend's neck.

That afternoon, an entirely new and revolutionary spirit marked the business session. The same men and women who were riddled with anger, defeat and discouragement 24 hours earlier were now discussing and developing a master plan to expand their efforts to take the Good News to the entire continent of South America!

You may be asking, "Is this really a miracle?" Definitely. It is a concert of miracles. I have studied human behavior from every angle and even at the graduate level: psychology, sociology, economics, history, political science, and theology. I have never read about or heard a therapy proposed that is capable of changing *a whole community* of 50 people this radically in just three hours. I know not of one behavioral dynamic that can bring a group of human beings to open confession, repentance, restitution, mutual sharing and bonding, and self-sacrificing beneficence in 180 minutes.

Yet one thing I am certain: there is power in the Spirit of God working through his Son, Jesus, in the hearts of those who are occupied by Him through faith.

It is the Spirit of God who makes life a miracle-walk for those who trust the Savior and allow Him to control and empower them. If you do not already believe, I challenge you to do so now and to surrender to Him.

"And all those who had believed were together and had all things in common; and they began selling their property and possessions and were sharing them with all, as anyone might have need."
Acts 2:44-45

———

Copyrighted material from *Miracle Walk* by Larry W. Poland, Ph.D., edited and used with permission.

Epilogue

The Prayer That Changed Everything

When I was a child, my parents brought me to church, and I am very thankful for it. Consequently, I've always believed God exists. As I shared in my story "Feast or Famine," it wasn't until my college freshman year that someone explained to me that God wasn't a passive Creator—a smiling "grandfather in the sky," or an entity that was only worshiped by going to church. God is alive; He is someone who loves me and created me to know Him personally.

I began to understand that my selfish choices (what the Bible calls "sin") separated me from a relationship with God. Even though I was overall a "good" person, being "good" could never be enough to restore my relationship with Him. But, being the gracious God He is, He provided a solution to bridge the gap: Jesus.

Through Jesus, I have come to know and experience God's love in a vibrant and personal way. God sent His Son, Jesus Christ, to die on the cross in my place, to pay the penalty for my sins, that I may have true freedom in Him.

That evening, during my freshman year, as this was made clearer to me, I knew I wanted to begin a relationship with Jesus. I knew this was missing from my life, and so I invited Jesus to live fully in my heart, and be my Savior and my Lord.

I prayed a prayer similar to the one that follows. If you are unsure where you are at with God, or have never had a personal relationship with His Son Jesus, I encourage you now to pray this prayer:

Lord Jesus, I want to know You personally. Thank You that You love me so much that you died on the cross for my sins. I invite you into my life and ask You to be my Lord and my Savior. Thank You for forgiving my sins— every single one of the mistakes I've ever made—and giving me eternal life. Change me, heal me and give me a fresh new start with You.

If you prayed that prayer, tell someone you know who knows and loves Jesus, or write to me, so I can help you grow in your relationship with Him.

**The power that you read about in this book
is not in the prayer,
but in the God to whom you pray.**

Prayer Was Never Meant To Be Complicated

➤ Prayer is just talking with God. Just like I love having coffee with friends and we take turns talking, God loves it when we talk to Him and listen to Him. He often speaks to us through His Word.

➤ Write down your prayers in a notebook, journal or on your computer, and be sure to date your entries.

➤ Search for and ask God to lead you to scriptures you can pray through (like in Psalms). Praying God's Word is praying God's will. Following is an example of personalizing and praying God's Word from Ephesians 3:18-19. You can pray this way for yourself or loved ones.

God, may I/Suzanne have the power to understand, as all God's people should, how wide, how long, how high, and how deep Your love is. May I experience the love of Christ, though it is too great to understand fully. Then I will be made complete with all the fullness of life and power that comes from You God.

➢ Most importantly, when God answers your prayers, thank and praise Him! Write down how and when He answered. When appropriate, share this with others.

**My prayer and hope is that you will see
God's "marvelous doings" in your life,
and you will have the courage
to share your story, as well.**

If you have been encouraged by these stories, the contributors and I would love to know. Please send us an email.

If you have an amazing story of answered prayer, and would like to submit it for a possible second book, please send it to me.

You may contact me at Suzanne@AmazingAnsweredPrayers.com

To read more comments about these stories,
and how they have impacted others, please visit our website:
www.AmazingAnsweredPrayers.com

Made in the USA
San Bernardino, CA
13 November 2014